Praise for Ann K. Schwader's poetry:

Ann Schwader, poet and "imaginer" par excellence, represents in her considerable mythopoeic art something at once remarkably novel and yet somehow reassuring despite her often dystopian vision. She deploys her craft and technique to offer us in depth a wide range of adventures, past, present, and future, whether alluring, distressing, or horrific.

—Donald Sidney-Fryer

The dark and enchanting verse of Ann K. Schwader weaves layers and labyrinths of wonder and beauty. Her work burns with language perfumed with mighty magic. It is not to be missed!

—Joseph S. Pulver, Sr.

Ann K. Schwader's intoxicating poetry is as authentically Lovecraftian as it is brilliantly original. This is poetry that is truly transporting. Superb!

—W. H. Pugmire

It takes more than mastery of rhyme, meter, euphony, and alliteration to preserve the emotional essence of the weird poetry of Lovecraft, Chambers, and Frank Belknap Long. Ann Schwader's poetical vision re-evokes the same senses of terror based on the weird prose she offers in rhythmical form. It is as though one is reading the dreams of a gargoyle.

—Fred Phillips, author of *From the Cauldron*

From early inspiration by H. P. Lovecraft, and later science fiction, Ann K. Schwader's own voice speaks ever more confidently and resonates with messages profound and relevant, universal and perennial.

—Charles Lovecraft

If Yog-Sothoth knows the gate, is the gate, is the key and guardian of the gate, then likewise, Ann K. Schwader's weird verse opens a gate to lonely places where the Words have been spoken and the Rites howled through at their Seasons. Schwader's verse—haunting, evocative, arresting in both conception and imagery—gibbers like Old Ones' voices on the wind, and like the earth that mutters with Their consciousness.

—Leigh Blackmore, author of *Spores from Sharnoth*

.

Twisted in Dream

Twisted in Dream

The Collected Weird Poetry of
Ann K. Schwader

Foreword by Robert M. Price

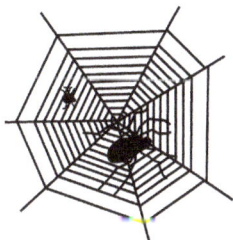

Hippocampus Press

New York

Published by Hippocampus Press
P.O. Box 641, New York, NY 10156.
www.hippocampuspress.com

Cover art: *Gothic* (2009) by Loretta Young-Gautier.
Interior illustrations by Steve Lines.
Cover design by Barbara Briggs Silbert.
Hippocampus Press logo designed by Anastasia Damianakos.

First Edition
1 3 5 7 9 8 6 4 2

ISBN-13: 978-1-61498-004-9

CONTENTS

FOREWORD

Many of us who dare to think we might do a passable job of pastiching Lovecraft's prose (and we may be overestimating ourselves!) would still balk at the very notion of imitating, replicating, his weird verse. Frankly, it would not occur to me even to try. How very astonishing, then, to witness the achievements of a very small group of Lovecraftian poets who deserve the name. And in the very first rank, along with the great Richard L. Tierney, is Ann K. Schwader.

This is inevitably going to sound more like a long promotional blurb than a true foreword, but I'm afraid that cannot be helped. For there is much to be admired, savored, in her work and nothing, as far as I can see, to criticize. I cannot finish a single poem of hers without feeling the creeping chill of Outsideness, of the eldritch Numinous that reaches out a taloned digit from Lovecraft's work to tickle and to graze us.

And this means that Ankh does not cheat the content, resting on the laurels of the form. Since most of us would find conformity to the classic sonnet and other forms such a labor, we might feel we had won a great victory if we got that far, and the meat on that skeleton might be pretty skimpy. And that would ruin the whole thing because the result would be ridiculous singsong. You will note: this is a lesson in the poetics of bad poetry, the kind Ankh does not write. But in the kind she does write, we discover the same effortless-seeming alchemy that we love so much in Lovecraft's *Fungi from Yuggoth:* the mixing of mind-expanding perspectives where science meets horror in their coinciding implications. And we realize, or we ought to, that the use of a classic, antique form (instead of, say, blank verse) to convey horrors undreamt of is the translation into poetry of Lovecraft's fundamental harmonic for weird fiction. The narrative must be restrained, mundane, like Pickman's brushwork, in order that the horror, when it arrives, may seem to burst through the worldly sanity of the narrative tone to sweep the reader away. This is precisely what Ankh has mastered. The delivery of a shocking revelation in the well-worn parchment of sonnets and other classic forms.

These poems might treat of pre-Lovecraftian themes, but even where they do, as in the thankfully many dealing with ancient Egypt, it is the antiquity that bears Lovecraft's stamp. And Robert Bloch's. But they flit like a hummingbird around the honeyed poison blossoms of the Mythos of Lovecraft and his school. And thus is another enchantment wrought. Many of us are Lovecraft purists, or at least we grant Lovecraft and his creations a priority so far above any other weird fictioneer that the Old Gent might as well reside alone atop his tall pillar like Simon Stylites. We cannot help regarding the presence of items of Derlethian lore (for example) in otherwise admirable Mythos tales as foreign matter cheapening the product. Ann Schwader escapes this. Like Tierney, she enjoys the post-Lovecraftian as well as the Lovecraftian and manages to incorporate both. Since her mood and technique are so faithfully Lovecraftian, the magic works. If I am typical of many readers, the reader will find Ithaqua, for example, tucked away here and there in these poems where one might have expected only references to the Mi-Go or some such to be at home. It is like a married couple: they are not united by blood until they combine genetic material to produce a child, which partakes of the flesh and blood of both, and at once the parents are blood kin by virtue of this extension of their "one flesh."

Finally, I note with relish how Ann Schwader has done what Lovecraft sometimes did, but in reverse. Lovecraft seems to have raided his own *Fungi from Yuggoth* sequence, as if it were a second Commonplace Book, as fund of story ideas. So we see both a poetic and a prose version, for instance, of "The Book." Well, so many of the poems in this collection have been built upon the plots and moods of various Lovecraft tales, then distilled into verse that one can easily imagine Lovecraft himself penning them. It is a great accomplishment.

Lovecraft, as you know, is quite dead. He will never give us another poem. I am very grateful to Ann K. Schwader for grasping up the fallen standard and providing a new mouthpiece for the Lovecraftian Muse.

—ROBERT M. PRICE

INTRODUCTION

As I write this, a resurgence of weird fiction is underway. H. P. Lovecraft is experiencing a surge of much-deserved popularity, anthologies of Lovecraft-inspired stories are springing up like eldritch fungi, and classic authors such as Bram Stoker and Mary Shelley are being discovered by a new generation. Yet there is no similar resurgence of weird poetry. Here in the twenty-first century, verse of any kind struggles in the marketplace, and the same readers eager to tackle a four hundred page anthology may balk at a sonnet sequence.

The question should probably be asked, then: What can poetry still contribute to the literature of the weird? Why should a modern devotee bother to read it, let alone write it?

Briefly, I believe the answer lies in the three Rs of Removal, Ritual, and Remembrance.

By its very appearance, a weird poem removes the reader from the mundane world of prose. Formal verse—still a frequent part of the tradition—only increases this effect. A poem on a page is visibly something Other. It cannot be skimmed, sampled, or summarized. It must be entered into on its own terms, temporarily separating the reader from his or her standard reality. The new one demands a more deliberate pace, a different and possibly alien mindset.

A weird poem is a gate.

Once that gate is opened, the reading experience becomes its own ritual. Poetry is language as it is not used in the ordinary waking world, as much chanted or sung as spoken. Like music, rhyme and meter can bypass logic and appeal directly to the primal. Since the reader is virtually hardwired for this approach, an atmosphere of the ancient, the mythic, or the cosmic can be established more quickly than it might be with prose—and maintained with fewer words.

A weird poem echoes the cave.

Long after the initial reading, those echoes of rhythm, rhyme, and heightened language make remembrance easier. Possibly too easy, or at least too effective. Is there any prose passage from weird fiction which sticks in the mind's ear at one A.M. quite the way Alhazred's "unexplainable couplet" does?

> *That is not dead which can eternal lie,*
> *And with strange aeons even death may die.*

So long as these lines are quoted by aficionados, I would maintain that weird poetry is earning its place in the literature. Although fewer modern readers are inclined (or perhaps prepared) to enter into a poem, those who do will still find themselves uniquely rewarded.

And inexplicably haunted.

—ANN K. SCHWADER

Westminster, Colorado
May 2011

Twisted in Dream

I.

MEMORIES OF THE WORM

- SL -
© 2011

The Worms Remember

When the legion marched on a Druid fane,
Defying the weird of an ancient bane,
& spilled Celt blood down altar stones
Till the barrows birthed revengers' bones;
When the eagles screamed to their last defender . . .
Under red earth, the worms remember.

All Hallows' Eve in Arkham town,
When the night watch hunted a wizard down
By prayer & candle, bell & book;
When they crept to his crypt & dared to look,
Then fed the ghouls all through November . . .
Deep in gnawed bones, the worms remember.

In the timeless ice of dead Kadath,
Beneath the gale of Ithaqua's wrath
Where frozen gulfs hide nameless things—
Unsleeping eyes & claw-tipped wings—
Where sanity turns sad dissembler . . .
Twisted in dream, the worms remember.

On a planet farther than nine we know,
At the system's edge where pale Mi-Go
Wing silently through twilight gloom

As the Old Ones plot Earth's promised doom
From whispered myth to cooling ember . . .
Silent as fate, the worms remember.

Out of Corruption

Those scholars who have read what they should not
Die fearing death itself far less than earth;
Each wizard's grave in some unhallowed plot
Is waiting cradle to a horrid birth.
Worms fed for eldritch eons on that diet
Of dark-fleshed knowledge fatten & grow wise
Beyond all wholesome comprehension—quiet
No more the ground where such rich feasting lies.

Exempt alone is he who seeks the pyre;
Or dies unwilling thus: a lifetime's lore
Turned ashes feeds the lurking worms no more
Than duller flesh which perishes in fire . . .
Or are precautions fruitless, after all,
When *things have learnt to walk that ought to crawl?*

     — after H. P. Lovecraft's *Necronomicon*

Power Failure

"Knowledge is power," the wise fool said,
Perusing Abdul Alhazred.
A Power came, but It found *him:*
The autopsy was pretty grim.

The Ghoul-Queen

Dark Nitocris, dread carrion queen
Who drowned her thousand enemies
At one great feast below the Nile,
Died mad, they say; & yet one sees

Strange spectres near the pyramid
Where priests entombed her still alive
For that . . . & other things she did
Which no soul human might survive.

At certain phases of the moon
(So runs the whisper in bazaars),
A *ka* wraith half invisible
Casts shadowwings against the stars

Then seeps away like incense-smoke
Below that same grim pyramid
To seek once more its parent clay
Where Egypt's primal stain lies hid.

There Nitocris & her dead liege
(Who once recarved the Sphinx's face
In terror of that Unknown One
Still worshipped in this lightless place)

Rule over those Osiris cursed:
Birth-freaks of the embalmer's art,
Who neither wear the forms of men
Nor beasts—but bear of each a part.

—after H. P. Lovecraft's "Imprisoned with the Pharaohs"

Out of Egypt

Necropolis stalker chaos-bred,
Yellow-fanged scourge of the Scarab's dead,
Ancient & awful as Khepren's doom
Ravaged by ghouls in his ruined tomb . . .
Lost prophets gibber his night-born name
Ageless & shifting as sand, or flame
Torn from the torment of dying stars
Held by a horror foretold as ours.
Out of dark Egypt's undying past,
Thoth's word of Making is fading at last:
Ebony entropy gnaws at our dreams,
Pharaoh of Shadows whose heralds are screams.

Abul Al-Hol

(Father of Terrors)

In Giza where the Nile's black secrets wind
Through vast tomb-cities ancient as this Earth,
A horror yet unknown to humankind
At large lurks in the hollow of its birth:
The man-beast Sphinx whose visage Khephren hewed,
Effacing features better left unviewed.

Grim guardian of necromancy's height,
It spans the sands beyond that pyramid
Where Khufu's lowest tunnels plunge toward night
& priestcraft's decadence long eons hid;
Those hybrid dead whose mummied forms portend
Dim elder gods of memory without end.

Strange soulless creatures! Ibis-headed men
Trail lumbering hulks of hippopotami
Whose human hands bear torches now & then
Down galleries where none can truly die,
Nor live . . . but only linger *in between;*
The courts of Khephren & his ghoulish queen.

Assembled by the thousands in one horde
Of leaping, creeping, shambling, shadowed Things,
They kneel with Nitocris & her dread lord
To sacrifice their nameless offerings
Before that rotted heart of Egypt's blight
Which gapes upon the final tomb of night.

What dwells within that crypt reveals no more
At first—small mercies—than its hunger dares;
The merest forepaw clawing at the floor,
Then padding catlike toward devotees' stares,
Supporting on its sprawling five-toed weight
The very terror crouched at Giza's gate.

—after H. P. Lovecraft's "Imprisoned with the Pharaohs"

Ech-Pi-El's Ægypt

Necropolis since Khepren's days,
Saracen gilt on a godlost maze
Twisted to mimic black wizards' ways . . .

Silent tread of the Sphinx's Beast
Down galleries where ghoul-things feast
On well-spiced meats of the elder East . . .

Pyramid midnights when *ka*-wings fly
On a murmured curse through moondark skies,
& magics live which cannot die . . .

Hieroglyphs graven in ageless stone
Quarried at last for a Pharaoh's throne
Where once They ruled . . .

& ruled alone.

Lord of the Land

Before Osiris rose to life-in-death,
One jackal shadow slunk around such tombs
As sorcerers command: strange-patterned rooms
Wherein the echoes of each final breath
Still whisper visions to eternal night.
Anubis heard—& hearing, laughed aloud
At fatal ignorance in those too proud
To host the humble grave-worm's final blight.

No simple jackal, he; but Night made flesh
Of senseless shadows & fear-maddened dreams.
The Thousand-Named, yet never what he seems;
Flawed pattern in this universe's mesh,
Dread Messenger of chaos & despair:
Nyarlathotep, who no life can bear.

Dream-Gates

Outside the harmless dark of wholesome sleep,
Grim wonders wait on mortals to destroy:
That Beast whose bloodthirst blemished Egypt's joy
In its young wisdom . . . secrets night-gaunts keep
Beneath their black-veined wings , . . what Hali hides
Amid its noisome waves . . . all these and more
Inhabit lightless lands beyond the door
Called Dreaming, & command their kin besides.

Those luckless ones who trouble nightmare's gates
Return not always untouched, nor alone.
From ebon heights where elder Things have flown,
They plummet earthward to a madman's fate
Of private torment to their dying days;
Learning too late *each dream-gate swings both ways.*

The Coming of Chaos

None dare to speak of it, & few suspect
That shadow-claws clutch inward day by day
(Too subtle for man's science to detect)
Upon this world still wobbling on its way
Between dim pasts in which it played no part,
& grimmer futures gnawing at its heart.

Our hierophants of physics little know
Dread Chaos bears a nearly human face:
Lean as the East where nighted rivers flow,
Yet lightless as that nether void of space
Where muffled drums & tuneless pipers laud
The mad gyrations of an idiot god.

This deity alone does Chaos serve
As lying herald & as messenger
Whose lightest word speaks nightmare down the nerve
Of all who hear . . . and hearing, might prefer

Their ignorance new-polished & pristine
To hinted knowledge twisting toward obscene.

Fresh shrieks of horror haunt the urban night,
Dreamstalked by darkside visions of some end
Crouched formless, nameless till the stars spin right,
Then shatter from the pattern they portend
Of tortured oceans spattered to the sky
By that which should not live, but would not die.

Thus reason treats with madness to survive,
& knowing skirts the borders of unknown
As Terra's erstwhile masters now alive
Deny whatever dust they claimed to own,
But—being mortal—merely held in trust
For Others who esteem them less than dust.

—after H. P. Lovecraft's "Nyarlathotep"

The Elder Lords

Alhazred dreamed them, at the last:
Their city old as Sarnath's doom,
Half-buried by an age of sand
Like bleached bones in a broken tomb;
Their walls so weirdly wrought & low,
Misshapen by geometry
Not of this world, nor any place
A mind less mad than his might see.

Theirs was no death-cult, though they raised
Strange altars to some nameless rite
In temples carved for crawling things
Who finally did not love the light;
But fled to paradise below,
Where hairless apes might never find
The last enigma of their lives.
Immortal, yes—& proud, & blind.

Their shadows stain the chill night wind
Whose grit erodes each bas-relief
They shaped as blazon to the years.
Their wraith-claws scrabble endless grief
Across the very sands they ruled,
Yet certain turnings of the Nile
Still bear their living eidolon . . .
Sebek, the sacred crocodile.

—after H. P. Lovecraft's "The Nameless City"

Out of the Nameless City

Beneath chill slivers of a silent moon,
Through streets which greeted Ib & Babylon;
A sand-wind snakes its moaning, tongueless tune
Of aeons past. Moreover, better gone.
Low temple passageways Alhazred dreamed
Exude suggestive tendrils of such breath

That even his mad mind awoke—& screamed
To learn the cursed impermanence of death.

No wandering Bedouin dares shelter here:
Deep desert wisdom ageless as the Nile
Still murmurs at the marrow of his fear
Of Elder Ones whom time could not defile,
But faded to a snarling & a cry . . .
Dim serpent-shades of hate which cannot die.

Asylum Sestina

At midnight star-winds carve into my mind
The hieroglyphs of long-engulfed R'lyeh,
Unspeakable dark image of Cthulhu
Spawned out of Chaos when the stars were ready
Till elder wisdom raised uneasy waters
Above these eldritch spires which hint at madness.

Small wonder I was driven into madness:
The bright configurations of the mind
Dim quickly in the depths of black-lit waters,
Convulse upon confronting dead R'lyeh.
No strength of human will alone is ready
Against the poisoned visions of Cthulhu.

Iä! Cthulhu fhtagn! Great Cthulhu . . .
Now chanting rises in some choral madness
To burst the Elder Gates & make all ready.

Some inner window of my shattered mind
Discloses dripping turrets of R'lyeh
Star-called from eons' death beneath the waters.

O, I have drunk deep of forbidden waters!
Alhazred's half-crazed scrawlings of Cthulhu
(The Waiting Dreamer couched in dark R'lyeh)
Laid plain the path I followed into madness;
Long study seeped its venom through my mind
Until the last page turned, & I stood ready.

Cursed be the night I held the gateway ready
& dared at last to gaze beneath the waters!
The merest dream-touch bared my quivering mind
Before the void-spawned horror of Cthulhu.
I shrieked myself into unquestioned madness
& woke to rave of star-signs & R'lyeh.

I hear Their voices calling from R'lyeh:
Throw wide the gate once more, the stars are ready.
Alas for this confinement of my madness
Which keeps me prisoned from the sacred waters!
Iä! Iä! Great Chaos-born Cthulhu,
Burst these last fleshly chains that hold my mind . . .

R'lyeh sleeps still beneath unquiet waters.
Ready at some far star-turning, Cthulhu
Sends dreams of madness, claims another mind.

Night Hungers

We speak of sleep as dread Nepenthe's gift
Turned toothless & benign—oblivion
On loan for hours only till the sun
Returns to call us back from that strange rift
Dividing life from death. Mad gamblers all,
To risk far more than reason understands!
This precipice we dare until we fall
Headlong is not some gentle Neverland,
But dissolution's doorstep. Brittle shells
Of selves (or souls) are merely that: mankind's
Illusionary games. What waits behind
The wall of sleep is every ego's hell
Made manifest . . . for Night, whose heart is Void,
Gapes there with mindless hunger unalloyed.

Hydra's Daughters

Such Lorelei as rise off Devil Reef
On May-Eve night or shadowed Halloween
Claim kin with no sweet mermaid ever seen
In wholesome oceans luring ships to grief.
No maiden marvels, these; but Hydra's brood
Spawned by old Innsmouth's dealings with the dark
Since Obed Marsh's time, that left their mark
In features more of fish than men, & skewed.

Their songs were never meant for human ear,
But summon Dagon's faithful to this shore
Where changelings of great age sometimes appear
By moonlight once . . . & then are seen no more
But dwell eternal in abyssal deeps
To serve that Lord who in R'lyeh sleeps.

Asenath: A Cautionary Tale (On the Doorstep)

She was a cursed & curious child—
A little weird, a little wild—
Who practically teethed upon
The dreaded *Necronomicon,*
For when it came to tempting fate,
Sweet Asenath could never Waite.

Her Innsmouth origins were foggy
(Some say her mom looked rather froggy),
Yet who could fault her doting dad?
Old Ephraim gave her all he had.
In fact, although his critics rue it,
He threw his very soul into it.

At Arkham's Miskatonic U.,
Some highly unkind rumors flew.
Her metaphysics were mediaeval,
Her whole appearance frankly evil,

Twisted in Dream

But who can question true love's dart?
She stole poor Edward Derby's heart,

Then set about with zest & vim
To sublet all the rest of him.
At shoggoth-pits and summonings,
Dark conversations with dead Things,
His borrowed bod's the one she wore.
No wonder Eddy D. got sore!

The moral, friends, is merely this:
If you would seek domestic bliss,
A Daddy's Girl is not the kind
To bring you lasting peace of mind.
For maids whose hearts belong to Pa,
Possession's ten-tenths of the law.

Inheritrix

When Britain's minions broke that cult of blood
Once spoken of in whispers as *thuggee,*
They little understood nor strove to see
What horror hailed such sanguinary floods.
Black-visaged Kali, Mother of the Void,
Lent Her grim image to this slaughter; yet
Some primal fear in man cannot forgot
An elder truth blind history destroyed.

*   *   *

Dark Mother, yes . . . but mother to such spawn
As creep beneath the earth & foul the night
In guises putting sanity to flight.
Fell younglings only Pickman might have drawn,
Though balking at the wellspring of that brood:
Shub-Niggurath, Black She-Goat of the Wood.

Mad Star Rising

There burns a certain star of nether space
Which shows but seldom in our mundane skies:
Seldom, & still too often. Human eyes
Were never shaped to view this alien face
Of cooling corpselight shedding flame like blood.
Its single cinder world retains no breath
Of any atmosphere, but only death
Drawn vacuum-stark in ancient lava floods.

Yet far beneath these plains of frozen fire,
A formless horror seeps, & shifts, & waits
For mortal dreamers' touch upon those gates
That open on the void of her desire . . .
The Magna Mater of all last mistakes,
From whose insatiate night no sleeper wakes.

Fear-Stars

In autumn when the Bull begins its rise
Red-eyed & rampant into midnight air,
No scholar steeped in lore & sorely wise
Stargazes then, lest his wide-searching stare
Should meet the gaze of dread Aldebaran—
No wholesome visage for the mind of man.

Mad vanguard to the haunted Hyades,
Carcosa's sanguine spectre of a sun
Enflames the misted shores which skirt Hali
Then sinks beneath . . . & as his race is run
Releases to the black stars of that sky
Hali's long-banished Lord who cannot die.

Meanwhile, above our own horizon's rim,
That same blood-beacon beckons through the void
To summon servants leather-winged & grim
Whose forms are neither fully humanoid,
Nor bird, nor bat, but that which Should Not Be;
The ice-rimed daemon tribe called Byakhee.

Far better on such nights to draw one's shades
Down tight against temptation, keep to thoughts
Of mundane mien—or wake, & lie afraid
Besieged by premonitions chaos-wrought:
Hastur Star-Stalker, on whose fell return
More than these mocking Taurus fires shall burn.

The Burrowers Beyond

Once living, lush, & fat with atmosphere,
Mars lures us by the riddle of its death:
Millennia carved deep, yet far from clear;
Flood-rutted plains where nameless things drew breath.
Nameless indeed, but not forever so . . .
Already mankind's fumbling touch begins
Against that sterile & protective skin,
Towards powers no race young as ours should know.

Mars died from inside out . . . is dying still
Of dread Wyrms ancient & chthonian
Imprisoned here before our minds began,
Yet reaching out in dreams to weave Their will;
Inspiring us to heedless, headlong flight
Toward that blood-beacon's signal in the night.

The Gate Between the Stars

In dark Na'morha, city of the Rim
Where Yuggoth's children swarm in ice-hewn halls,
A twisted archway towers high & grim
Above obscenely rune-encrusted walls.
The trapezoidal stone before it shows
Black stains of sacrifice from eons past
Against the shrouded pale of methane snows,
& nighted ranges infinitely vast.

Twisted in Dream

The first explorer to defile this place
Will no doubt seek within the gateway's void
For evidences of some Elder Race
Who raised that arch, & carved that trapezoid . . .
The manner of his passing will be known
By fresher tribute spilled upon the stone.

The Wind Beyond

In deep November's flawless onyx skies,
Through certain interstices of the night,
A wind may slip whose origin denies
All ordinary boundaries of fright;
Some breath of deathless menace from Outside
Chill as the cavern-gales pale shantaks ride.

Those last leaves lingering in treetops speak
Strange secrets then, deranging wholesome sleep
With horrors old as Hali, & as bleak
As that unspoken name black waters keep
Beneath the dim light of a dying star
In Taurus where the air-lord's daemons are.

Such winds as this call snow from high Kadath
To heap corruption on the crisping lawn,
Some frozen fragment of that Walker's path
Whose passing brings fresh dread each winter dawn

Beyond those clement lands where sane men go:
The territory of the Wendigo.

In deep November's flawless onyx skies,
Through certain interstices of the night,
A wind may slip whose origin denies
All ordinary boundaries of fright;
Some breath of deathless menace from Outside
Chill as the cavern-gales pale shantaks ride.

Night Terrors

When twilight deepens into gaping dark,
& rends that fragile veil of ignorance
Which shields us from discovery's fatal spark;
Gaze not at length—or suffer consequence
Star-spawned, star-cursed. These cheerful lights we greet
Hold ageless malice mired within each heart:
Unspeakable dead dreams of Man's defeat
On gibbering winds to gnaw a world apart.

Our lives upon this rocky pawn of Fate
Are safest passed both deaf & blind to all
Beyond the bar of gravity's iron gate.
To question farther risks a certain pall . . .
The horror-deafened ears & maddened sight
Of one who stared too closely at the night.

Night Terrors II

(Of Cosmic Curiosity)

Beyond this placid island in the void,
Our science fumbles with impatient hands;
As children grasp at flame they must avoid,
& learn by burns of nature's bleak demands.
Yet Saturn's siren-rings still harbor worse
Than that which seeped to Earth & dim N'kai;
The mines of Yuggoth mask their buzzing curse,
Our Moon's own lifelessness remains a lie.

Between these worlds & weirder, shadows wing
On pinions scaled . . . or methane-rimmed . . . or bone;
Aldebaran in Taurus holds someThing
Whose very *name* is better left alone—
Small wonder crawling Chaos smiles & waits,
& by his daemon Sultan lays more plates.

Moot Question

Higgledy-piggledy
Lovecraft in Providence
Thought Elder Evils crawled
Out of the sky

What with defective planes,
Third World nukes, acid rain

Nobody's asking old
HPL why.

Night Glyphs

Scrawled on our skies from the outside
night glyphs
divide mere dark from greater shadow
deride our island ignorance
in letters bled
from fire

In the beginning (they mock) was Chaos
pure & idiot & perfect
a daemon sultan's waking dream
defiled by clots of stars

The whimpering of solar winds
cannot disguise His primal piping
pale flickering of primate lives
cannot defy His elder children

Scrawled on our skies after midnight
hieroglyphs
eulogize the death of order
trigger cracks within the mirror
each mind reflects
come morning

Of Stonehenge & Star-Myths

These sacred sarsen circles hold no light
For modern priests of mordant academe
Secured by ivory ignorance from fright
Raw-edged & primal as a newborn's scream,
Yet blind as that same babe to wisdom old
As any pillar on Salisbury's mold.

Midsummer sunrise o'er the great Heel Stone
Defines the outer limits of their view:
This henge was built by primitives alone
(So they believe), & plotted by them, too.
Thus stumble fools along one narrow path,
All ignorant of Yoth & grim Kadath.

Before Earth's merest primate rose to climb
That fragile ladder Darwin later traced,
These lands & myriad others lost to time
Spawned sorcerors unchained by hour or space
But gifted—cursed—with pure & lethal Sight
Which pierced that mercy-veil we call the night.

Yuggoth they knew, Celaeno & beyond
Where Azathoth's mad minions trace their dance
In supernovae. Limitless gulfs yawned,
Admitting things that left this world no chance;
Except (if even then) by noting well
Which faint star-movements heralded such hell.

So rose great marker stones upon that plain
Which holds them still, yet holds their secret, too;
Passed into dust until none can explain
How warnings might be charted here . . . nor Who
Drifts dreaming in that black beyond the black
Which these rude guardians were ranged to track.

Barrow-Walkers

Unquiet plain of hunched & tumbled bones,
When nightmists rise along each chalky ridge,
What shades betray thy fearful heritage
Of grave mounds aged beyond the great henge-stones?

Unleashed from barrows turfed by centuries,
Pale Neolithic spectres greet the moon
As ancient cousin; raise their primal tunes
On that same bonechill wind the living flee.

Unwholesome haunt such elder mysteries keep,
What daemon-rune defends thy quiet days?
What word of power works its subtle ways
To scatter shadowkind toward troubled sleep?

No human guardian turns back this curse,
But raven legions each new sun reveals,
Reminding those whose flesh once made their meal
How succulent *souls* are . . . as they disperse.

The Last Betrayal

Naked & shaking in our dim cave's cold,
We grope with prayers & prophecies of light
Along cerebral corridors. *Foretold*
We term *forewarned,* & map the very night
(Which elder wisdom feared as mystery)
With prying instruments incessantly.

This process we call science, fate, or faith;
According to our era & our pride.
The more we map, the deeper we can hide
From primal terror stalking like a wraith
Through sepulchers to all we thought we knew
Scant generations past—then found untrue.

Yet in the end, this very arrogance
Which sends us blind & stumbling into space
Shall prove no more than fatal ignorance
When mystery meets mankind face to face
& strips the stars from dazzled human eyes . . .
Revealing Void that all about us lies!

Auld Leng Signs

Young Akeley, final scion of his line,
Brought back from Arkham shards of Lengish glass:
Pale clouded souvenirs without design

Through which (if one stared long) strange shadows passed.
No knowledge had he of the Hyades,
Celaeno, Yith, or Yuggoth on the Rim;
Yet trial & error showed him all of these,
Until his ignorance caught up with him.

Toward midnight at the closing of the year,
His worried friends broke down his study door.
They found glass fragments splintered on the floor,
A severed tentacle, *one reddish smear,*
& knew (as they ran shrieking from the spot)
That auld acquaintance might best be forgot.

The Companion

No printing press detailed my chosen gate
Through timelost vortices of space & dream;
But human hand haled into dust too late,
The crabbed transcription of a silent scream
Still echoing. Unprized & cheaply sold,
That tome's remains reshaped my inner sight;
Turned Now to Past, & darkness into light
Bled from some dying star gone red & cold.

Nor do I wander these weird realms alone:
Transition's price is shadow, unto death;
A dread companion lacking life or breath,
Yet craving both for reasons of its own . . .

Dogs howl me, for their nerves cannot abide
This nightside stalker unseen at my side.

—after H. P. Lovecraft's "The Book"

Tonight on the Late, Late Show . . .

Where scholars read by lanterns in the night
Of ancient wisdom ghastly & obscene,
Their children now revere the household Screen
& sprawl like fungi in its pallid light.
Unschooled in thought, unversed in mythic tomes—
Von Junzt, d'Erlette, or darker Alhazred—
They gape before this gate of eldritch dread
Thrown open from Beyond into their homes.

Shrieks shatter midnight as black digits grip
Through glass at souls, drag victims to the void:
Nyarlathotep's cursed fellowship
These ignorant young minds cannot avoid.
No mortal strength unaided will deter
This medium become . . . the Messenger.

Night Lives

Beyond staid confines of this waking shell,
Sleep sets our souls to rove among the stars.

Algol's demonic gaze that hints of hell,
Dread wyrm-curse coring out a dying Mars . . .
All these & weirder fill our eyeless sight,
While scented music filters through such spheres
As poets strive to sing of morn & night,
Yet spend their toil for little more than tears.

Unbound by flesh, we slip both space & time—
Behold the Sphinx's birth, or grim Tsan-Chan
Three thousand years ahead in history's span—
But pay in bitter coinage for our crimes:
Dream-shreds too thin & fleeting to relate
Are all our minds retain at morning's gate.

—after H. P. Lovecraft's "Beyond the Wall of Sleep"

Life Studies

His art illumed no otherworldly space,
No blood-lit moonscapes touched by Klarkash-Ton;
But now he is mysteriously gone
& fearful colleagues turn from his disgrace.
His brushwork scarcely matched the skill of Sime:
Exotic, never; only stark & clean—
Yet in its very clarity obscene,
Unblinking witness to unnatural crime.

What canvases of his they found, they burned.
Those few surviving tell a stranger tale:

Lost genius striving far beyond the pale
Toward madness. Best his critics never learned
Of that sealed cellar with its ancient well
Where Pickman drew *from life* the face of hell!

—after H. P. Lovecraft's "Pickman's Model"

Moon-Fears

I traced the twistings of that moontouched stream
Where lotos-faces whispered as they died
Down changeling vales until I stood beside
A long-drowned city risen out of dreams.
Unwholesome yellow beams revealed each spire
As ornament of some necropolis,
Yet hid one final secret: worse than this
Crouched waiting for my gaze beneath the mire.

What I had taken for a sprawling reef,
The ebb tide forced unveiled upon my sight . . .
I turned away in sickened disbelief
To seek the squirming shallows till sunlight
Might sear my memory of what dead face
Adorned the ancient Guardian of that place.

— after H. P. Lovecraft's "What the Moon Brings"

The Gatekeeper

Not in the mundane space we know,
But in the void *between*
A Gate there is—a Gate He is
Which keeps seen from unseen.

Before we crawled from primal slime,
Or crafted tools to kill,
The Old Ones seeped from stars beyond
& bent Earth to their will.

Their cravings raised cruel citadels
From Ocean to Kadath:
Across stark slates of stone & sky
They scrawled Their alien wrath

In runes no man alive may read.
Earth did not suit Them wholly,
& so They ceded mastery
To hairless apes too lowly

(Thank all dark gods!) to use such scraps
Of lore as They might leave . . .
So those who wish to sleep at night
Unplagued by dreams believe.

Though They departed in the flesh,
Their essence yet remains;
Too subtle in its structuring
For our weak apish brains

To gaze on it—or Them, perhaps—
Without the aid of learning
Which once in wiser times sent scores
Of wizards to their burning.

Their voices mutter in the deeps,
& gibber on the wind;
Their footfalls fault the solid rock,
Force cities toward their end,

Yet none behold the loathsome cause
Of this & that disaster:
They lie in wait beyond that Gate
Who is time/space's master.

Yog-Sothoth is the key & ward
Who holds the spheres apart;
The Gatekeeper & Gate in one,
The dagger at Earth's heart.

He knows which routes the Old Ones took
To rule this spinning mass
Of rock & slime . . . & at what time
Mankind's brief rule must pass

Into the mindless jaws of night
As Elder lords returning
Raise ancient walls against the flame
Of ape-built cities burning.

Not in the mundane space we know,

But in the void *between,*

A Gate there is—a Gate He is—

Which keeps seen from unseen.

Sarnath Remembered

In Ilarnek's great temple squats a Beast

Enshrined with gold & lapis, & with fear

By shattered men recalling Sarnath's feast

Of victory-turned-death, its doom writ clear.

Few worshippers frequent this idol's place,

Still fewer view his priests without some dread:

'Tis rumored these cowls hide no human face,

But shroud the seeming of a race long dead.

Yet when the moon shows gibbous in the lake

Which sheltered those of Ib (*who were not men*),

Both priests & people gather here to make

Respect to one who ruled, & rules again

In shadowed lands beside a stricken shore

Where Sarnath's marble ramparts rise no more.

—after H. P. Lovecraft's "The Doom That Came to Sarnath"

In Memoriam Arthur Jermyn

Not all life's hidden horrors lie between
Unhallowed depths of space & hollowed earth:
Humanity itself holds much unseen
That's better so; yet brooding toward some birth
Through science into hard, unblinking light.
Self-knowledge beckons, but that adder's kiss
Secretes a lethal venom banned by right
Of sanity to memory's abyss.

The merest mirror glimpses may suggest
Some denizen of daemon-ruins lost
Beneath the Congo's dark unquiet breast . . .
What price self-knowledge now? What fearful cost?
So simple silvered glass may prove a curtain
Cruel as spider-silk, & as uncertain.

—after H. P. Lovecraft's
"Facts Concerning the Late Arthur Jermyn & His Family"

A Man of Many Parts

Young Herbert West of Miskatonic U.
Revered recycling . . . of the human kind,
And bent the morbid brilliance of his mind
To bringing off what only gods may do.
His early errors raised some local fuss
(The Sefton madhouse keeps its secrets well),

But this was nothing to the later hell
When Dr. West got really serious.

He came home from the War a shattered man.
Too much fresh meat, too little research time?
Alas, the opposite. His darkest plan
Crept back from France to answer crime with crime,
A danger all researchers learn to dread:
Consumed by Science, Herbert lost his head.

—after H. P. Lovecraft's "Herbert West—Reanimator"

Yule-Thoughts in Kingsport

Along these streets hung thick with fragrant boughs
I walk in dread, recalling elder rites
Our fathers made of evergreen & light
On strange shores mercifully forgotten now.
Each holiday well-wisher's face I scan
With nightmare apprehension . . . could this shell
Shaped cunningly in counterfeit of man
Conceal what no sane human tongue may tell?

Toward midnight, when the ancient church is lit
Wherein *their* festival was kept before,
I clutch at talismans & bar the door
Against ancestral memories that flit
In shadowshapes of madness through my head:
Things living still, which should have long been dead.

Twisted in Dream

The Whippoorwills

Shrill psychopomps, they haunt the shadowed glens
Where strange survivals of New England's past
Still whisper in the twisted dreams of men
This world is theirs, & humans not the last
To conquer here . . . fell birds, whose voices rise
& fall with every failing mortal breath;
As though to coax a soul from dying eyes,
Yet rend from it all hope of wholesome rest!

No deathbed spirit in this dreadful place
Escapes unscathed; save one, whose blighted birth
Alone revealed his less than human race:
Half wizardspawn, half nothing of this earth.
Winged watchers scattered to the skies, & cried
Wild panic on the night young Whateley died.

—after H. P. Lovecraft's "The Dunwich Horror"

Lavinia in Springtime

(Sentinel Hill)

albino girlchild
gathers pale daisies under
ancient stone dolmens
loves me loves me not loves me
dark thunderheads clustering

Stargazing Along the Miskatonic

Horror from the stars
seeps down through rifts of madness
on night's horizon:
Aldebaran, Celaeno,
icerimmed dark wings approaching . . .

Untimely Observation

Beset by missiles since its merest birth,
Our battered pebble wanders through the dark
While we, the self-made monarchs of this earth,
Deny the day when one will find its mark,
Dethroning us forever. Although signs
Lie scattered thick through certain ancient texts,
Some imp of the perverse—nay, the malign—
Preserves our ignorance of what comes next.

No common rock awaits our soil, but seed
Of nightmare's primal myth: those nameless Ones
Who raised up unclean empires while our breed
Still bubbled in the mud. Though other suns
Have fallen to them since, there's no disproving
The stars are right . . . & one of them is moving.

Sestina: To the Audient Void

He came to us a lean & shadowed stranger
From out of Egypt, ancient root of nightmare
Branching into thousand-visaged chaos.
We did not know him for a messenger:
He spoke of science, seldom of the gods.
We never understood that we were lost.

His comprehensive grasp of knowledge lost
Before Atlantis drowned was strange—yet stranger
Rumors named him acolyte to gods
Long banished from this planet, star-spawned nightmares.
We scorned such superstitious messengers,
Preferring the technology of chaos.

The least of his devices reeked of chaos,
Yet our intelligentsia were lost
Within their ivory egos, messengers
Self-referential. Useless. Any stranger
Might retrofit our city into nightmare
Beneath the noses of these tenured gods.

Sophisticated past the reach of gods,
We found ourselves instead embracing chaos
In darkened lecture halls where tri-dee nightmare
Crawled from the screen to scavenge what we lost
Through long immersion in this sea of strangers
Preoccupied with signs & messengers.

The more we listened to this messenger,
The less we comprehended. Demons, gods,
Or aliens (perhaps all three, & stranger
Than myth itself) insinuated chaos
Within our dreaming minds till hope was lost
Of any sleep that did not end in nightmare.

Our city's nights became a public nightmare,
Yet when our council dispatched messengers
In search of foreign cures—some wisdom lost,
Perhaps, with our abandonment of gods—
They came back madmen. All, they raved, was chaos;
The human order shattered by a stranger.

I am the lost . . . the last . . . the messenger
Of nightmare & those mindless, formless gods
Served by the crawling chaos. Farewell, stranger!

                            —after H. P. Lovecraft's "Nyarlathotep"

Neighborly Whispers

I heard them in the woods again last night,
Those voices whose inhuman, buzzing tone
Erased all doubt that we are not alone
Upon this rock. Half paralyzed with fright,
I understood as I had not before
What blasphemous infinities extend
Beyond our skies, & what those gulfs portend

Now that our science scrabbles at the door
Of ignorance. I heard . . . yet woke to find
My world much as I knew it in the past.
Small comfort! For in every neighbor's speech
I recognize some strange & subtle breach
Suggestive of abyssal realms too vast
For Einstein's theories, or my peace of mind.

—after H. P. Lovecraft's "The Whisperer in Darkness"

If We Return

We thought a spangled rag & footprints made
This rock our property. Not so. We left
Too hastily to call it more than theft
Gone sour, raw delinquents so afraid
Of dark & death & cold they bolted. Now,
Long decades later, here we are once more—
Not even slightly wiser than before,
Still asking *if* we should much less than *how*.

Meanwhile, that second lunar face we meant
To get around to someday wakes at last
In shadows bred for blood & vacuum flight.
They swoop with unmistakable intent
& shriek inside our minds that Man is past,
These Byakhee of interstellar night.

The Darkness Whispers

(Flagstaff, AZ 1930)

Again tonight, the search for Planet X
goes on, though Lowell's gone these fourteen years,
& Mars Hill sure gets lonesome in the dead
of January. Tombaugh aims the 'scope
toward Gemini's black interstices, hoping
for two good plates in three, some hint of motion
beyond bleak Neptune lurking at the rim.

Beyond the rim of human comprehension,
the darkness whispers . . . & strange aether wakens
to speed the journeying of Those Outside.

Almost a month slips by before those plates
claim his attention. Sifting, shifting stars
& asteroids like sand grains in his eyes,
he stares into the blink comparator
until a single pinprick in the background
reveals / conceals / reveals its affirmation
of everything that Lowell died believing.

Of everything belief can teach of demons
when outer darkness whispers, so men's dreams
reveal the lineaments of Those Outside.

The news of Planet X—soon Pluto—breaks
on Lowell's birthday, though his mausoleum
sleeps mute as ever in the stubborn snows
of spring at altitude. Tombaugh delivers

Twisted in Dream

the word himself—then lingers, puzzling
at footprints sunk bear-deep, but pincer-clawed
like some crustacean foreign to this earth.

Like some tongue foreign to our waking minds,
a darkness whispers: Yuggoth, new-found Yuggoth,
the outpost & the gate of Those Outside.

"—and I wish, for reasons I shall soon make clear, that the new planet be-
yond Neptune had not been discovered."
      —H. P. Lovecraft, "The Whisperer in Darkness" (1930)

Wide Enough

Wide open space, they call it. . . wide enough
For mysteries our cities crowded out
Long generations past with light & doubt
& science. Only landscapes like these bluffs
Of barren sandstone, plains of sagebrush hold
Reminders of remoteness past the stars
We humans know of; unsuspected scars
Left here by Others, terrible & old.

Most folks ignore what they can't understand
Mind their own business on a cosmic scale,
& so for now the status quo prevails
Though ancient energies besiege this land,
Soul-chilling & persistent as its wind:
The clawing of the Outside wanting in.

Elder Signs

Pecked into windswept stone with sweat & blood,
These icons of a farther, stranger place
Hold history grown dim before the Flood,
Eternal malice with a primal face.
Serpents, pipers, multi-legged beasts
Betray the shapes of entities unknown
Since Earth's first days, when They arrived to feast,
Then stayed to dream in cities of their own.

No key survives in modern minds to read
What's written here, & so the experts term
Them mysteries of spirit, nothing more.
Nothing like a warning—or a door
Cracked wide enough to show what darkness squirms
Among the cringing stars to make them bleed.

Ancient Echoes

(Chaco Canyon)

There is a silence here which time alone
Cannot explain. These oddly angled walls
& broad roads built for reasons past recall
Are thick with wisdom older than their stones,
Arcane as nightmare. Shadows gather fast
Despite the heat, & certain passageways

In ruined kivas hint of darker days
Too long eclipsed by mankind's mayfly past.

Deserted, surely. . . yet the shifting light
Of dusk & dawn wakes echoes in this place,
The sibilance of shades unsatisfied
By mere mortality. Past wrong or right
Or frailties of flesh, they spawned a race
Which never left at all—*& never died.*

The Ones Who Come

Midsummer, & the thunder speaks tonight
Not only from the heavens, but *below:*
A tremor through this land we think we know,
All ignorant of underlying fright.
No coyotes raise their voices to a sky
Bruised deep by lightning prophesying rain
For once unwelcome, harbinger of pain
No human comprehension justifies.

Best now to bolt the doors, try not to think
What fell to earth here once, & what it brought
Across some unimaginable brink,
The mind's event horizon. Long forgot,
Yet near at hand, They rise upon this storm—
Wind-twisted spectres of no earthly form.

Faint Echoes

(Pyramid of the Moon, Moche)

Within these ruined walls, an ocean lies,
Though no such ocean as the earth has known.
Both bright & dark at once, its art defies
All expectation of what may be shown
& what must not, for sanity's own sake,
Reveal itself to any mind awake.

Grim lord of all this mythic painted sea,
One figure out of nightmare dominates.
His alien gaze repeating endlessly,
Enwreathed by tentacles, suggests the fate
Of captives as an octopus's prey:
Exsanguinated, slaughtered, tossed away.

Yet such zoomorphic rationales cannot
Eradicate the whisper of a fear
Forged by atrocities our world forgot
Before the first ape stood—yet drifting clear
As corpse-scent through this dim miasmal air,
An echoing of madness & despair.

What drove the Moche priests to draw their knives
Across the frantic pulse of human throats,
To fill their chalices & drink the lives
Of men like sacrificial sheep or goats?
Ancestral memory . . . ancestral dreams . . .
& deeper still, a deathless Dreamer's schemes.

Inhuman, mutter archaeologists,
Not fathoming the truth behind their words:
Star-spawned survivals veiled by legend's mists
& rituals which mercifully obscured
Their origins with horrors too mundane
To seed suspicion in a scholar's brain.

Within these ruined walls, an ocean waits
In token of that ocean set with stars
Though dark between them as this planet's fate
When His black city rises from some far
Abyssal exile to proclaim its place
As mortuary temple to our race.

*"After all, the strangest and maddest of myths are often merely symbols
        or allegories based upon truth . . ."*

—H. P. Lovecraft, "The Shadow over Innsmouth"

Blood Calls

Blood calls us from night's shores into a dream
Of underwater glories, strange & deep
As coral labyrinths where shoggoths sleep,
Or long-drowned fanes whose gilded priesthood schemes
To wake a dead god from beneath the waves,
& rise to harvest tribute which He craves.

Blood calls us from the prisons of our minds
Too earthbound fragile to appreciate
The machinations of ancestral fate
In sinew, flesh, & bone toward that design
Most prized by Those who swam between the stars
Incalculable lifetimes before ours.

Blood calls us to old Innsmouth's haunted streets
Once home to hundreds of our sea-born kin
Who fell by treachery, yet live again
Within our mirrors—till, the change complete,
Our mothers' mothers welcome us below
To learn what only Earth's next masters know.

Shunned Things

Men bury what they dare not understand,
But never deep enough. Its poison rises
From unacknowledged graves in strange disguises,
To wrest from living flesh the dead's demands.
No wholesome vegetation burgeons there,
No live-born babe draws in a single breath,
While darker energies undimmed by death
Bleed vengeance-tithings from the very air.

So fared the daemon taint of Paul Roulet:
Though slaughtered by his fellows out of fear
& superstition in a stricter day,

The ebon essence of his soul fought clear
Of earth's restraints to rise unfettered . . . maim
The lives of generations with its blame.

—after H. P. Lovecraft's "The Shunned House"

Jaded

I long to learn of wisdom found
Through mildewed tomes locked underground
In wizards' lairs & ghouls' retreats,
The haunts of Si'lats & ifrits.

I crave that esoteric lore
Which blotted stars out long before
R'lyeh withdrew beneath the sea
To threaten dreamers' sanity.

I have a passion to peruse
The inspirations of that Muse
Who whispered low in Geoffrey's ears
& spurred young Edward Derby's fears.

Away with texts mundane & tame!
I thirst to know each nameless Name,
The hieroglyphs of Irem's tombs,
The lost details of Sarnath's doom,
The moon-rites of the restless dead . . .
I want to read what Alhazred.

Less Famous Last Words

Shrieked a Nantucket sleighriding crew,
There are some things no whaler should do!
If you hunt Devil's Reef,
You're just begging for grief:
It's not what you'll harpoon, but Who.

Doorway to Madness

Spine cracked
like a racked witch,
its covers creak open,
disclosing some idiot god's
dark jest.

Not Alone

We're not alone, or so the theories go:
Infinities of worlds exist—all real—
That multiverse our quantum wizards know.

Tomorrow, they may learn enough to steal
Like mice through some convenient cosmic crack,
Or even open one themselves, reveal

But here the mind of science fades to black.

Whatever utter Otherness awaits
Our ignorance, there'll be no going back,

No bolt to shoot across those shattered gates,
No epithet to equal our distress
(However brief)—no record of our fates

Who might have turned aside, content with less,
& cried to all dark gods for loneliness.

Star-Turn

(an acrostic apocalypse)

We dwellers in these infinite black seas
Hold tightly to our island ignorance
Eroding from the possibilities

No science can deny. This dalliance
Too soon—too often—must exact its cost.
Horrendous past imagining, to chance

Even the vaguest understanding! . . . Lost
So hopelessly to wholesome blindness, all
To gain mere data! Whether holocaust

Approaches from the void, or dripping walls
Rise up from deep R'lyeh to ravage dreams,
Such correlated knowledge speeds our fall

Certain as the stars disclose Their schemes
Of resurrected sovereignty. To seek
Much further might advance the last extreme:

Extinction of our species. All these bleak
Revolving gas-balls augur is no more,
In truth, than that mankind is young & weak—

Given as prey to Those who came before,
Huddled a moment only on this shore,
Till Yog-Sothoth reveals both key & door.

The Quiet One

Her neighbors rarely notice her at all.
She tends her garden, keeps her cottage neat,
& regularly occupies a seat
At Sunday services, so there's no call
For them to venture past that soft gray wall
Of silence. Past her prime, though vaguely sweet,
She blends into the bustle of their streets
& disappears. It's only in the fall
When stark October settles like a doom
On fields & town alike that she reclaims
Her elder self: the rituals she learned
In other lives, the manuscripts—& tombs—
She pillaged for the knowledge of such Names
As would have once condemned her to be burned.

Darkest Mother

Spawner of shadows too twisted for Earth,
Harboring havoc unleashed with each birth . . .
Under the razor of May-Eve's thin moon
Black Ewe's teeming progeny bleat out a tune
Noxious & mindless as Azathoth's own
Incarnadine fantasies raving alone,
Gazing through flaws in the fabric of space,
Grasping for minions to master our race
Unknown, unheralded—young from that womb
Ravished by primal Night, gravid with doom
Ancient past prophecies—bane of mankind,
Thousand-faced horrors to harry our minds
Headlong towards madness, defenseless & blind.

Handmaidens of the Worm

They rise like night mists from the charnel ground
Whenever fresh-dug earth spreads out its scent
As spoor upon the wind. Where graves are found—
From sepulcher to humblest monument—
This sisterhood of shadows soon appears
To sample what the worms might only waste,
Dereft (as they are not) of many years'
Appreciation of acquired tastes.

*   *   *

Dread Ammut's daughters all, the rite they keep
Is final in a sense no priest may claim.
Defilers of eternity's dull sleep,
They worship Hunger by Her eldest name
& honor with their thrice-corrupted breath
Her ceremonies of the second death.

The Coming of Ammutseba

Before this ball of mud we call our world
First sprouted peaks above primeval sea,
Before Earth's constellations first unfurled
Their cryptic hints of some mythology
Too vile to comprehend—too chaos-fraught—
Chaos Incarnate spewed a random thought.

At once the tuneless piping of His thralls
Fell silent as their master's implications
Made manifest . . . malignant . . . stalked those halls
Where space & time form twin hallucinations;
The ravings of a ruined consciousness
Divine in scope, self-prisoned by excess.

Alas, that intimation soon escaped
To foul the purity of mundane space,
Where mindless matter waiting to be shaped
Combined with mad intent to curse our race's

Ancestors with flame across the sky
Of lost Lemuria where legends died.

No lifeless meteor, but seed of Night
Esurient soon rooted in that land.
Wild sacrificial blazes set alight
By torches clutched in tentacles, not hands,
Allayed a god-thing's craving for those fires
Which spatter midnight with celestial pyres.

Such meager sustenance could not suffice
Forever. As this thought-spawn's hunger grew,
Its first devotees paid a fearful price:
No longer would mere heaps of timber do.
To simulate the tang of astral sparks,
Live immolations cauterized the dark.

At length, invaders claimed this place instead—
Stone altars superseded seared earth-fanes
To honor that same Presence out of dread
& hope commingled cringing in the brain,
As faith itself has ever been defined
Within the gray straitjackets of our minds.

These complex creatures pleased Its appetite:
Scarce more than apes, yet still of wizard-breed,
The raw necrotic power of their rites
Permitted It to grow—& growing, feed
Upon the life-force of their enemies
Like summoned fever, conquest as disease.

So *hubris* must have seemed to tragic Greeks
World-wise & weary, centuries advanced.
Lemuria's crude sorcerers could speak
Of nothing similar . . . nor any chance
That stormwracked night when mountaintops spat fire
Till heaven shattered, at their god's desire.

*   *   *

Some few survived, of course. Some always do,
Two-legged rats embracing any spar
Worm-riddled to the heart or rotted through,
To keep their seed afloat. What evil star
Smiled on their diaspora is unknown:
They traveled shadowwise, & not alone.

The shoreline of that nighted current Styx
(O innocents to come, who sang it Nile!)
Put forth a plague of temples, death-cults mixed
With elder rituals which once defiled
Ten thousand worlds whose dust forever drifts
Between the snags of interstellar rifts.

Nyarlat, Seth Kinslayer, Shuddam-El,
Horemkhu, Azathoth, & other Names
Best left unspoken on this side of hell—
All these they celebrated without shame,
Yet in their atavistic practice sensed
Some lurking unappeased malevolence.

Twisted in Dream

No formless horror now, It chose the guise
Of goddess—Nut Sky-Mother—from these minds
Manured well by priestcraft; but devised
Pernicious variances in design,
Decaying astral jewels to cankered scars
Adorning this Devourer of Stars.

Thus *Ammutseba*'s worship spread its blight
From Delta southwards to the cataracts,
Extinguishing in Stygia all light
Of lesser deities who dared attack
Her architects of twisted paths worn deep
In nightmares poisoning our planet's sleep.

Nor was Her cult exclusive to mankind:
Those dwellers in the deep sands who emerge
By twilight only, alabaster blind
From aeons in the dusk, revered this scourge
Of bright perdition as their own godhead.
(Inevitably, they & humans bred.)

*   *   *

Long centuries along this tainted border,
The sweeter seed of Kemet slowly grew
To raise up sanctuaries which, though ordered
By Stygia's grim mythos, honored too
New avatars of light: great Amun-Ra,
Fierce Sekhmet, & Maat's eternal law.

Yet darkness is a thing which cannot die,
As power is a madness all its own.
Before three human dynasties had passed,
A wizard-pharaoh sacrificed his throne
Upon Nyarlat's altar of seduction;
Strange wisdom bartered for a world's destruction.

Black land ran scarlet now beneath Thoth's moon,
& Seth-winds from the red land wailed of death,
Until Sneferu's soldiers (none too soon)
Prevailed; though even with his fading breath,
Nyarlat's entombed cat's-paw prophesied
A horror still to come, *whom stars would feed.*

Now pyramids reached high on Giza's plain
As monuments to more than mortal pride;
Khephren's recarved colossus spared his reign
From features better not identified
Too accurately . . . but portents of hell
Failed utterly when greater Darkness fell.

*   *   *

A certain pharaoh's reign wore on apace,
Past strength of arm or will or common sense;
Until his vizier, lacking wisdom's grace,
Endeavored to restore his lost puissance
By sending sweet young flesh to spice his bed:
A maiden rescued from the sands half-dead.

She spoke her name *Sesh'tet,* a whispered sound
Like serpent-winds across those parched red lands
Where Stygia still flourished underground
& wove its sorceries with hybrid hands.
O graceful as a priestess! Pharaoh cried
(For once, his purblind vision had not lied).

So Ammutseba's covert votary came
As harem-ornament, slim serpent coiled
In Pepy's failing bosom. Kemet's shame
Grew nightly as mephitic shadows soiled
Its spotless moon & scarred the very sky,
While minions of the light began to die.

Before her pharaoh's *ba* had safely sped
To join the once-imperishable stars,
Black Nitocris seized kingship in his stead
Until her vengeance-craving went too far
At one great sacrificial banqueting
To pleasure Powers only blood will bring.

Soon Giza's high-peaked tombs no longer rose
Inviolate beneath the night's protection.
Bipedal jackals ravened where they chose,
Destroying any hope of resurrection
Except for Khephren & his shambling train,
Who served the Sphinx's avatar of pain.

Throughout that tortured century, Her cult
Of ghoul-tongued heresy & madness spread

Among those nameless vermin who exult
In plundering both living flesh & dead . . .
Uncounted pharaohs faltered on the throne
Of Memphis where Maat's last truth had flown.

*   *   *

Undying young, Sesh'tet rewove her will
Like spider-silk ensnaring any man
Who risked the double crown of Khem . . . until
Some lost celestial balance tipped again,
& Mentuhotep marched to gratify
His Theban war god with a cleaner sky.

Soon temple steps in tarnished Memphis ran
With blood enough for even Sekhmet's thirst,
As Montu's chosen soldier-king began
Restoring order to a land accursed
By Stygian malice older than mankind;
A Darkness veiled by feminine designs.

One morning at the apex of Ra's flight,
A squad of stern-faced priests searched that *harim*
Where Sesh'tet plotted heresies of night
& hauled her out at last. Her mortal screams
Rose up like incense on the desert's breath
As offering to One who savors death.

They left her body where the sands drift deep,
Rare carrion for jackals to devour—
Yet even famished creatures fled such sleep

As this. Through all the fading gilded hours
She lay untouched, until basaltic gloom
Brought shadows to conduct her to her tomb.

Ten sevens of long days & nights they toiled
With arcane instruments, by rites unspoken
In any human tongue. Rich-spiced & oiled,
Her wrappings bore that hieroglyphic token
Of Ammutseba's ultimate regard:
Her daemon-text, the *Gate of All Lost Stars.*

Far west of Thebes, secreted in their shrine
Like knotted maggots at Earth's heart, a horde
Of hybrid mummies welcomed to their line
This high priestess of primal dark. Ignored
While empires ground themselves to dust, they waited . . .
Then Tutankhamun's gold was excavated.

II.

ANCESTORS & ACOLYTES

The Weighing of the Soul

When Nephren-Ka, Black Pharaoh of the East,
Came to the Scales wherein men's hearts are weighed,
The very balance shook as though afraid
To judge against Nyarlathotep's priest.
Fierce Amemait-Devourer-of-Souls
Lost appetite before such tainted meat,
Anubis howled a beaten cur's defeat,
Thoth blotted his cartouche from Egypt's rolls.

Among these petty gods an elder rose,
Whose face their nightmares knew as one of dread;
He lingered but a moment—till they chose
To make him a fear-offering of the dead.
The Mighty Messenger, his mission done,
Led from the tomb his hierophant . . . and son.

> —after Robert Bloch's "Fane of the Black Pharaoh"

The Tomb of Nephren-Ka

Coiled under Cairo's ageless heart it waits
For seven thousand years to cycle past
Until Earth shudders at the Blind Ape's gates
Burst open to unleash cursed truth at last,

The aimless flailings of such Destiny
As no sane mind should ever crave to see.

Dread Nephren-Ka dared more at Egypt's height:
Usurper-prince of sorcerers & priests,
He fled the common blessing of Ra's light
To wrest strange wisdom from the long-deceased.
Anubis howled aloud . . . but Sebek smiled
Reptilian relish at the land defiled.

One god alone this darkest Pharaoh served,
Displacing all the Nile's great pantheon
With temples to that Mighty Messenger
Whose shadow fouled the stars in ages gone—
Nyarlathotep spread his daemon-fame
From Memphis to Irem in blood & shame.

Prophetic prowess was the poisoned boon
This Messenger bestowed . . . at hideous cost.
Thrice-glutted jackals bayed a bitter moon
In Nephren-Ka's bleak empire of the lost
Till desperation festered into war,
& temple steps ran black with wizards' gore.

They razed his name from every monument,
Effaced it from Thoth's roster of the dead,
Yet still that shadowed Messenger had sent
Some solace to his hell-cult & its head:
A secret palace-tomb torn deep in stone
Where Nephren-Ka might claim his promised throne.

Twisted in Dream

One hundred priests went willing to his blade
Before his last ambition came to be.
Death-fevered sharer of immortal shades,
He filled the very walls with prophecy;
Mad truths inscribed in flawless black & white
From Egypt's birth until her final night.

Coiled under Cairo's ageless heart it waits,
Yet no man living claims its hidden lore;
Those heedless souls who seek the Blind Ape's gates
Soon hold their heathen peace forever more . . .
Fresh stains beneath these walls recall the price
Of Nephren-Ka's last horrid sacrifice.

   —after Robert Bloch's "Fane of the Black Pharaoh"

Namesake

In dread K'n-yan's spired citadel, Tsath,
Where Yig & Nug are honored without awe
& decadence holds sway in place of law,
There yet remains one fear-forbidden path.
The onyx staircase winding down from Zin
To black N'kai lies broken now & barred
By tortured fragments of an undead guard
In token of the terrors housed within.

Tsath's sole expedition to that place
Left few alive to tell of what they found:

How viscous entities without a face
Lived sightless centuries beneath the ground . . .
& how the Thing they worshipped was the same
As that which gave Tsath its once-proud name.

—after Z. Bishop's "The Mound," as revised by H. P. Lovecraft

The Old Ones Whisper

in their high lost canyons, chipped flint chitterings like a thousand bats rumored to shelter from the lethal heat here. Rumors, indeed. Rumors raised against madness. These night legions unfolding from ancient cratered walls are not & have never been bats, nor anything warm & mortal. Their daylight murmurs hold more of primal chaos than of nature, & the prey they crave in their silent hunting is not spoken of aloud.

Now sleep the Old Ones, sing the Tewa in their pueblos. The time of their working is past.

But the wisdom of the Tewa is the wisdom of scant centuries. Of hard-baked earth & calloused brown flesh. The knowing of the Old Ones stretches back like the zigzag bulk of Awanyu, feathered serpent rain-bringer/father, infinitely twisted through time & space & dream. Back to the flawed beginning with its senseless spatter of stars. Forward & forward & forward till even that idiot spewing makes sense . . . hideous sense . . . & the Old Ones flit chittering through canyon shadows no longer.

Far away now their children are, sing the Tewa.

And so they remain—for now. For as long as wind & rain spare these crumbling walls, these crude stone-peckings so meaningless to modern eyes.

Twisted in Dream

Only so long. Even the Tewa do not remember why certain glyphs were first carved, or what waits coiled between the stars until they fade. But the Old Ones do.

And the Old Ones still whisper.

[Tewa quotes from *Songs of the Tewa,*
trans. Herbert J. Spinden, Ph.D.]

Yig Country

Low tom-toms throbbing through the autumn air,
Shrill Pawnee whistles rising day & night,
Alert the learned traveler to beware
Of this cursed region's legendary blight.
Dark-rumored Yig devours now all men
Who harm his hissing children . . . that, or worse;
For whispers reach the ear now & again
Of victims who survived Snake-Father's curse.

Drive on to cleaner country if you're wise,
Ask at the Guthrie madhouse if you must:
There's little wholesome to the human eye
Still wriggling in its basement straw & dust,
But evidence enough behind one door
That sane researchers will inquire no more.

— after Z. Bishop's "The Curse of Yig," as revised by H. P. Lovecraft

Survivals

In Anasazi lands where ruins rise
Like gaping spectres up the canyon walls,
Faint petroglyphs still strange to human eyes
Mark mysteries forgotten by the Fall.
Awanyu feathered serpent writhes among
The eldest glyphs, yet by another name
He slithered from the stars when Earth was young:
Great Father Yig, of K'n-Yan's shadowed fame.
His worshippers built well here in this place;
& fed well, too, on certain nameless meat
(For they were of K'n-Yan, & past disgrace)
Until their failing faith called down defeat.
They live here still, cursed by Yig's broken trust,
As rattlers hissing mindless in the dust.

Drums of the Father

Dread autumn brings a throbbing on the wind
From lost Tenochtitlan to Santa Fe . . .
A gnawing at the margins of the mind,
Reminders of a darker ancient way.
The first folk of this land, who used to pray
At Yig's deep temple-burrow in K'n-Yan,
Learned well the rites which kept His curse at bay—
Then brought them to the sunlit world of man
As knowledge in the blood, past faith or plan.

The wisest keep them so, afraid to guess
(& rightly, too) just how these drums began.
O wholesome ignorance! for they express
A primal horror words cannot impart:
The slow reptilian echoes of His heart.

Guardians of the Mound

In Caddo County where the snake-god's rite
Still haunts September souls, a hillock stands
Warded by apparitions day & night,
Twin tokens of an elder tribe whose lands
Are ours but briefly. Dawn reveals a brave,
While twilight sends a headless squaw to pace
By pallid ghost-light . . . &, perhaps, to save
The ignorant who might attempt this place.

A third & grimmer guardian attends
Those luckless few who persevere. Their fate
Is mirrored in these mangled odds & ends
Of flesh—unliving & yet *animate*—
From one who sought to challenge Those Below,
& suffered torments only madmen know.

—after Zealia Bishop

Pompelo's Doom

(a dream of Chaugnar Faugn)

Before Rome's restless eagles worked their will
To claim the cursed & craglost Pyrenees;
Before, indeed, its storied seven hills
Were more than mud beneath primordial seas;
A thing of Chaos twisted time & space
To manifest Itself among our race.

The Greeks & those before them knew It well
As feeder, man-beast, eater of the all,
As shadows in the dawn, or sudden pall
Across the stars at midnight . . . shape of Hell
Incarnate, yet with contours ill-defined
To any but a wise & troubled mind.

At length It & Its lesser brethren came
To plague Iberia's high wilderness
With toad-spawned servitors by loathsome name
Of *Miri Nigri,* shaped as men but less
Than puppets for each horrid act & thought
That Its inhuman chaos-mind had wrought.

Each Kalends of November brought such rites
As nightmare shrieks of on the mountain crests
Above Pompelo: all that life detests
Was danced & drummed of in those black delights,
Until great Rome, in sickened sympathy,
Sent aid to its beleaguered colony.

One cohort of the finest marched that day
Against a foe no Roman blade could mark—
In pride & ignorance they wound their way
Amid strange hills until the falling dark
Revealed too late what made their horses scream
Brute terror at the madness of this dream.

What howled & gibbered on those hellish peaks,
No man returned alive & sane to know. . .
What roused the hills themselves to prey below,
Pompelo's colonists could never speak
Without a rolling eye, a mouth of foam:
Dread Chaugnar Faugn, who broke the mind of Rome!

—after Frank Belknap Long's *The Horror from the Hills*

Confession of the White Acolyte

From lost Tsang to Lhasa's ancient gates,
I bore the bane of Mu Sang's prophecy,
Soul-bound since time forgotten to one fate:
To nurse Great Chaugnar over land & sea.
I dared not hurl my burden to the waves
In dread of sacramental vengeance . . . cursed
Indeed my coward's life! for courage saves
Us not from death itself, but from the worst
Which lurks beyond that vale. Damnation deep
As any traitor's is my portion now—

Unspeakable, unhealed, I rise from sleep
To rue the mirror's verdict on my vow,
& read within the ruins of my face
The dissolution of the human race.

—after Frank Belknap Long's *The Horror from the Hills*

The Shore of Madness

On wings of alchemy I chased the past
Through ebb & flow of all humanity,
Beheld Atlantis vanquished by the sea,
Then backward further still—until at last
The simplest single cells winked out of sight
As angled time replaced the purer curve
Of mundane being. Stricken to the nerve,
I glanced about in light that was not light
& found myself upon the *other side:*
That ghost-gray shore where silence writhes & shrieks,
Where there is never anywhere to hide.
A wind is rising now that steams & reeks
Like daemon's breath . . . dear God, I know those sounds . . .
The nightmare baying of Tind'losi Hounds!

Twisted in Dream

Art Imitates, All Too Well

Higgledy-piggledy
Klarkash-Ton artisan
Mirrored wordSmithing in
Carvings & paint:

Arch-fiends from Averoigne,
Zombies of dead Zothique . . .
Who's game enough to peek?
Brother, I ain't.

The Fane of Mordiggian

There is one god alone in Zul-Bha-Sair:
His sacred law, revered past that of kings,
Condemns the city's dead to seek his lair,
Bereft of ease which earth or flame might bring.
Both meek & great must offer at the last
Their mortal leavings for the god's repast.

His priests go muffled through the shadowed streets,
All argent-masked in likenesses of Death.
Their purple robes are mockingly discreet,
Their passage silent as a panther's breath.
O foolish are those few who follow when
They bear strange burdens from the world of men!

Like some great worm that gnaws the city's heart,
His temple crouches in the midst of all
Yet seems a thing so utterly apart
That sun may never brighten, nor night pall
These walls of adamantine shadow raised
To that dread lord whom kites & jackals praise.

Within, his laden altar stretches wide
& black as Hades, lit by flaming urns
Revealing what fresh cerements ought to hide.
Here sacrifices ripen, each in turn
Awaiting that unspeakable embrace
Enfolding those who tarry in this place.

Four doorways gape upon the sunlit world,
Yet townsfolk seldom venture far within
& fear upon their souls that curse unfurled
When body-snatching wizards stoop to sin.
Necromancer . . . *heretic!* . . . despair:
There is one god alone in Zul-Bha-Sair.

—after Clark Ashton Smith's "The Charnel God"

At the Yielding of Twilight

Eternal shadow shrouds these tombs
We tryst among, as time devours
Even such dim & furtive hours
As sleep may spare us. Rare perfumes

Twisted in Dream

Of necromantic lotus blooms
& all Nepenthe's sacred flowers
Call forth dream-loves more real than ours
From ancient glories, storied dooms.

Our passion gutters like those sparks
Which once traced legends overhead
But now burn low, their blazons furled.
We linger lonely in the dark,
Envying beloved dead
Who danced upon a younger world.

—after Clark Ashton Smith's "From the Crypts of Memory"

Rede of the Gray Weavers

(fragment)

Fold down thy limbs & tremble, fellows of Tch'tkaa!

O clever weavers of Abyss who follow
That winding wyrd of web & pounce & prey,
Who suck soul-marrow from thy enemies,
Who vault above the void of dying stars,
Abase yourselves!

For all your fine-wrought weavings are as nothing
Before the glyph-web spun of Atlach-Nacha,
Voormithdreth's dark dweller in the gulf

Who strains this writhing world between his strands
Of adamantine law & ancient night.

Recall that star-bridge strung from Cykranosh
Which Atlach-Nacha wove to bear the bulk
Of Lord Tsathoggua when They came
In elder aeons—how the Voormis shrieked
To see that spangled scar across their sky!

Consider how in Voormith's sunlost depths
The final pattern of this earth's demise
Is worked in subtle silks hung thick with skulls:
So end as merest husks all heretic
Intruders on His dread & holy toil . . .

—after Clark Ashton Smith

Voormi Hymn of Deliverance

Hail to thee, Sfatliclllp! Great Mother-Sister
Who shared with us the primal seed of stars,
Who lent Thy holy body to our cause,
Bestowing thus upon us one who raged
Insatiate & ravening as flame
Through all the proud streets of Commoriom!

Hail to Thy spawn, Sfatliclllp Avenger
Who tumbled down these jungle-vaunting walls,
Who shattered human spires of arrogance,

& fed Thy children well on their pale flesh
When tempest-like Thou drove them forth in hordes
To die lamenting in the wilderness!

Hail to Thy might, o Sfatlicllp Merciful
Who lurketh in Eiglophian murk forever,
Who nurtureth Thy folk in high wild places
As cubs unto the sanguine saber-tooth!
Preserve in us Thy sure & Protean puissance,
& grant deliverance by Thy ancient blood.

—after Clark Ashton Smith

Postscript: *The King in Yellow*

Soul-sick, I laid aside that slender text
(Its serpent binding slithered from my hands),
& sought the healing ease of sleep—now vexed
By tainted wisdom's hideous demands.
Black stars betrayed the region of my dreams:
I traced Cassilda's path along that shore
Whose poisoned mists obscure forevermore
Deep Hali's nameless horror. Shattered screams
Rang echoing from dread Carcosa's towers
Where nothing human dwells, nor ever dwelt
In twisted cells where disembodied Powers
Still make themselves most maddeningly *felt*.

Too late, I knew that tortured voice as mine,
& woke to see I clutched . . . the Yellow Sign.

—after Robert W. Chambers et al.

A Phantom Walks

Along the yellowed edge of urban night
Frayed thin by cynic pride & decadence
Near decade's end, there prowls a pallid fright
Whose aspect cries demise to hope & sense.
It masks as Truth, yet wanders featureless
As newsprint still uninked, or static screen;
Twin images of media distress
At Truth turned fading phantom. Such pristine
Temptation lures us all into a mist
Now rising thick as Hali's haunted breath:
The subtle horror of the mind's slow death
Made comforting. Wake, sleeper! To resist
Alone preserves us from that Phantom's fate—
The jaundiced tatters of his King who waits.

—after Robert W. Chambers et al.

Autumn, Lake Hali

clawing the cloud waves
ebon skeletal fingers
                    flap yellow tatters

Stargazing, Lake Hali

black stars staring back
from those mist-shrouded waters
your soul slipping in

A Lost Song of Cassilda

Carcosa's final sunset dies,
& I alone send up this tune
Beyond that shore where cloud waves rise,

For Death has veiled my sister's eyes
To mock the mist-enshrouded moons.
Carcosa's final sunset dies

As Truth distains his pale disguise;
Men's thoughts which stretched through afternoon
Beyond that shore where cloud waves rise,

Recoil as they attain their prize:
Our royal father's jaundiced rune.
Carcosa's final sunset dies

While black stars desecrate the skies,
& whippoorwills displace the loon
Beyond that shore where cloud waves rise.

My soul shall taste its own demise
& trail funereal tatters soon . . .
Carcosa's final sunset dies
Beyond that shore where cloud waves rise.

Evening Reflections, Carcosa

(Camilla's Song)

Cassilda sings the dying twilight down
Again to me tonight from her soul's tower
Remote now as Aldebaran: lost bower
Consumed by shadows, Truth's last phantom flown
Out of remembrance, though she knows it not.
She is our last to bear that pallid mask—
An ancient bane named *Life;* our last to ask,
Aching & heartsick, after long-forgot
Surrenders of the flesh. By what design
Our tattered sire desired her to endure
Centuries above . . . no ebon water

Redemption in Hali for this damned daughter
Adrift in Hastur's halls, I am unsure,
Cursed as we all are with his bitter Sign.

A Queen in Yellow

Inscribed upon a thousand tattered leaves,
Carcosa's autumn lingers on the wind
Like threnodies a fading daughter grieves
For dynasties denied—or underpinned
By shadows of that truth whose pallid mask
Portends a question worth her soul to ask.

This land grown ancient in its sorceries
Shall know no further season, save a chill
Enlivened by the rising Hyades
Into a winter endless as that will
Which seized upon Carcosa from the start,
& etched one bitter Sign within its heart.

No footsteps but her own now haunt these streets
Where wizards triumphed . . . & Camilla fled
Before that prophecy which yet repeats,
Though all save one who honored it lie dead
In Demhe's clouded depths where specters rise
With glitterings of midnight in their eyes.

Immured within a swirl of tattered leaves
Whose saffron susurration hints of things
Hali shall hide no longer, she achieves
Her father's throne at last as twilight sings
Those tears she left unshed, & cloud-wave mist
Shrouds this necropolis his signet kissed.

                              —after Robert W. Chambers

III.

AFTER INNSMOUTH

I. Flight

Fear-driven as a beast, I fled that place
Where moonlight summons horrors from the sea:
Time-twisted hybrids of some ancient race
Whose every line suggests what Should Not Be.
Through underbrush & clumps of thorn I crept
To bring at last to Arkham my mad tale
Of elder rites thought dead which only slept . . .
Grim government men listened, growing pale.

The night they dropped torpedoes off the Reef,
I woke still shrieking. Fire engulfed my dreams;
Yet deeper waters drowned their futile schemes
& stirred in me recallings past belief.
Though Innsmouth's dying now, it leaves behind
Long shadow-marks of doubt across my mind.

II. Discovery

My mother's brother traced our Arkham line,
& killed himself soon after. Now, two years
Since Innsmouth's hell-soul spread its shade on mine,
I know the secret wellspring of his tears.
Our great-grandmother . . . *what* was she, & how
Did Obed Marsh's madness taint our stock?

The truth of it arrives in nightmares now;
My thoughts turn darker daily with the shock.

Last night again I swam to Her below:
Twice-great-grandmother, daughter of the sea
& star-spawned Others alien to me . . .
My waking self distrust such scenes, although
His visage in the mirror makes it plain
What sent the bullet through my uncle's brain.

III. Decision

Too often now, this inland night wind brings
Salt-scented prophecy from Innsmouth's shore;
The whispered conversation of such things
As cannot die; or did, yet live once more.
I must not live at all: a pistol waits
Beneath my hand to end this sea-spawned voice
Which tempts me from my death with grander fates.
I strain—but cannot make my uncle's choice.

Iä! Y'ha-nthlei! City of our blood
Where ancient kinfolk call for my return
To long-drowned altars where strange votives burn
For Him who dreaming waits beneath the flood . . .
My journey to your depths begins tonight
To serve immortal till the stars turn right.

IV.

CHARLES DEXTER UNWARDED

- SL -
© 2011

I. "Who Shal Looke Backe"

An antiquarian from infancy,
He roamed the dreaming streets of Providence
In utter & aesthetic confidence
That what had been might not yet cease to be.
Its gambrel roofs & ancient seafront smote
His whole attention from those early days:
No winter sunset wove its mystic haze
From Prospect Terrace westward without note.

Yet even as he yearned to reach the past,
The past reached him by pathways most malign.
Ancestral evil stained his mother's line
With darkness death itself could not hold fast,
But only wait upon some fated one
To raise its shape again beneath the sun.

II. "Of Whither He Voyag'd"

Down London streets & dim Parisian ways,
He traced strange specters of unwholesome lore;
Befouled his nights, & squandered youth's bright days,
Yet ever pressed ahead in search of more.
Mediaeval Prague revealed its maggot heart,
Cruel Transylvania's craglost heights as well;

By age-veiled ritual & shadowed art,
He forged himself the very keys to hell.

Great Europe's secret sewers of lost thought
Spilled forth for him, till home alone remained
Untainted by the terrors that he sought.
Small comfort! Sorceries still deeper-grained
Awaited Charles' return to hearth & hall:
That poisoned portrait on his study wall.

III. "Do Not Calle Up . . ."

By word & sign & symbol old as Death,
By rune & ritual of banished Night,
He wrought the final weirdings of that rite
By which dead things aspire to life & breath.
Dogs howled his folly to a fainting moon
On that grim April night when history failed
To hold its gravelost own, & spells prevailed
Against the grasp of nature late & soon.

No painted scrutiny beheld this feat
Of conjuration: Curwen's portrait curled
To dust that night . . . yet through this luckless world
A shudder ran. From history's defeat,
A victor rose to mock mortality
With such survival as should never be.

IV. "From Dead Saltes"

His bungalow above Pawtuxet shore
Concealed deep knowledge ageless & profane,
A cellar shambles—nay, all that & more—
Where fearful wisdom trickled from such brains
As ghouls delight in. Riven from their sleep
By necromancers' craft & outright threat,
The hallowed dead no grave could safely keep
Surrendered all in horror & regret.

Blind error wrought its worst therein, yet still
Brought forth one former victim to defend
A foredoomed land from madness without end.
Thus ill sometimes must counter greater ill . . .
Unaided, no man mortal might displace
Undying malice masked by youth's mild face.

V. "Of Humane Dust"

Time sends some ending to all sorceries,
& Nature is not mocked, however bent
By ancient art or hideous intent.
All dust of ages craves some cleansing breeze
To sweep it from this waking world toward rest
Untroubled & eternal: each man's right
Of passage on this plane is short, & night
Falls equally upon the worst & best.

So Curwen learned, by curse of Dragon's Tail
(Descending node of necromantic fame).
His conqueror, though tremulous & pale,
Transcended darkness by a single Name
Wrenched from that void where death & life mean less
Than mocking & chaotic nothingness.

V.

PICKMAN'S PROGRESS

I. Admiration

There never lived, nor ever (God!) shall live,
A painter Pickman's equal; not if fate
Is merciful to fools, or may forgive
Dark knowledge gained too strangely & too late.
No mythic moonscapes marred his view of hell:
Detailing sharp-edged as a shriek of pain
Carved out such denizens of crypt & well
That fellow artists shunned him as insane.

"Ghoul Feeding" marked the final blasphemy
For most, but my regard craved stronger meat.
How could mere brushwork capture—nay, repeat—
Such features of fear's physiology?
Yes, thus I praised with unsuspecting breath
A genius spawned of dealings worse than death.

II. Revelation

His rented house in old North End held things
No modern wall might harbor, or inspire.
New England's witch-nights lit by charnel fire,
Pale scavengers subway disaster brings . . .
Yet none surpassed the ghastliness half-wrought
On canvas in his cellar studio;

A horror so alive, so clearly caught,
I feared the artist lost where madmen go.
Would that I thought so still! A single slip
Of paper pierced that theory, & my mind;
One snapshot I forgot to leave behind,
Then glanced at—as devotion lost its grip
Against stark evidence turned epitaph:
His *model* glaring from that photograph.

III. Encounter

Now Pickman's gone, but not so far as I
Could wish him in these wan & nervous days
When darkened cellars spark a fearful cry
& mad ambition's echo haunts my ways.
At dusk upon the waterfront I spied
His half-familiar features peering from
A pile of rags. I stopped—& nearly died
Disclosing what that genius had become.
These weeping wounds along my arm were torn
By nails once fouled by paint alone. No more!
Black tears of torment mingled with fresh gore
Sustaining something human once, but born
Anew in shadow to perdition's part . . .
A life in imitation of his art.

VI.

LAVINIA

"Lavinny's read some, an' has seed some things the most o' ye only tell abaout."

—H. P. Lovecraft, "The Dunwich Horror"

I. Forgotten

No signboards point the road to Dunwich town,
& whippoorwills bewitch the fading light
In lieu of human voices. Snaking down
These strange domed slopes, a river gleaming bright
As sacrificial steel affords no song,
But murmurs in the marshy depths below
Of times long past . . . & of survivals strong
Beyond the mundane span most mortals know.

One such still lingers near that altar-stone
Upon the barren crest of Sentinel Hill:
A pale, misshapen wraith who drifts alone
Just as she did in life—yet by her will
Made flesh, this region bears a ghastly fame,
Though few still living recollect her name.

II. The Female Line

Old Whateley's wife came of an ancient stock
Abhorred in Salem centuries before.
Inheritors of *Al-Azif*'s grim lore,
They fled the stake, the gibbet, & the block
From Britain into wilderness—yet found
Their kindred here as well. Blood called to blood,

Until dark prowess crested in a flood
Of wizardry. The hills for miles around
Reverberated with their daughter's birth:
Her father heralding this pallid mite
As sign more certain than the stars come right
That those Outside should rule again on earth;
Her mother shrieking at her own decline,
For power passes through the female line.

III. Child of Shadows

Her father's books were all she knew of school,
This child of shadows, secrecy, & dust;
But they sufficed her. Girls learn what they must
& as they may, for destiny is cruel
To those unfit to face it. Page by page,
Two centuries' inheritance revealed
A cosmic paradigm best left concealed:
The dissolution of our human age.

Her mother, too, had heard the siren song
Of Dee, Von Junzt, & others of their kind,
Yet perished by a dire miscalculation.
To discipline her daughter's prideful mind,
She thought to test her—till the spell turned wrong,
Resulting in her own incineration.

IV. Predestined

She heard the voice of thunder in the hills,
& knew it for a summons. Wandering
Alone among the ageless stones, she thrilled
At premonitions subtler than spring
Might spark in other maidens. All she'd read
& wondered at came clear, as though a gate
Had opened for a moment in her head,
Revealing her both cursed & fortunate
Past human comprehension. Lightning split
The sky in triumph as she turned for home
Convinced of chaos & her place in it,
Exulting in the mystery to come
Beyond this last brief spate of April rains:
A black tide rising, surging in her veins.

V. May-Eve

No swan wings here. The storm that took her screamed
All night like demons stooping to their prey
Somewhere beyond the sky, & sleepers dreamed
Of cities crushed to history. As day
Seeped back through bloodied clouds, a lone girl made
Her way along a twisted hillside path
To face her father's scrutiny, afraid
She'd failed his teaching, earned a wizard's wrath . . .
So Leda's legend faltered in the face

Of Otherness determined to break through
In its own season. By this vessel, torn
& yet transcendent, something would be born
To rend the fragile veils of time & space
Till void unending burst upon the blue.

VI. The Other One

No husband to her name! The gossips' tongues
Wagged ceaselessly, though she seemed not to hear
Their spite well-leavened with a secret fear
Of who—or what—had sired her goatish young.
Murmuring above his dusky head,
She crooned him prophecies of eons past
Yet still to be, with his own future cast
Across them like an avatar of dread.

Those few who overheard could not suspect
She sang for two, & not this child alone.
Within the Whateley attic, floorboards groaned
Already as an appetite unchecked
By limitations of this earth craved more
Each day of mutton, beef . . . or human gore.

VII. His Father's Voice

His first All-Hallows' Eve, & yet he ran
Before her to the summit all the way,
Delighting in such rites as wizard-clans
Have kept for centuries to speed the day
Of Their ascension. Sky-clad without shame,
They danced among the stones on Sentinel Hill,
& kindled fire at midnight to proclaim
Our past & future masters passing still
Unseen among us. Silhouetted stark
Against those flames, her boy's physique revealed
His heritage—& as she raised her dark
Ecstatic chant, the clouds above congealed
In thunderclaps to make the child rejoice
With intimations of his father's voice.

VIII. Locked Out

Their callers often found her all alone,
Surrounded by the tattered scraps of books
Her son had little need of, being grown
Already quite the scholar. When her looks
Turned strange & sullen, or she muttered words
Not meant for men to speak, they edged away
As though the fleeting time had just occurred
To them: could business wait another day?

Secure again in solitude, she mused
At length upon the sounds & stench which bore
Down from that upper story. Without doubt
Her father & her . . . offspring . . . could have used
Her gifts as well; yet when she tried the door,
They'd locked it from the inside. Locked her out.

IX. Whippoorwill Night

He was her father, yet his dying eyes
Slid past her own to settle on the lad.
Bearded at eleven, hulking, mad
For hidden wisdom: had they been unwise
To teach so much, so young? The midnight hills
Groaned their reply . . . & as her father's breath
Seized in his throat, cacophonies of death
Burst from a thousand waiting whippoorwills.

"They didn't git him." True enough. The birds
Fell silent in an instant—yet she knew
With all her truest Sight she'd lost him, too,
& stood without protection on this night
Of shifting balances. Without a word,
She hid herself away until first light.

X. Final Signs

He had no use for her, & made it clear
In half a hundred subtle, heartless ways.
Too wise for warning & too blind for fear,
He kept her from the ancient sacred days
To offer fire alone on that bleak hill.
His books—once hers—stayed under lock & key,
But certain notes she found provoked a chill
She recognized too clearly: *this shall be*.

The Bishop woman, trying to be kind,
Bewailed the wretched waywardness of sons
Till she could stand no more, & spoke her mind
In desperation. What her boy had done
She couldn't say, nor what he thought to do . . .
Each sleepless night, she wished that it were true.

XI. Hallowmas Rite

She snuffed the lantern when her son had gone,
& waited for the whippoorwills to flock
In all their dusky prescience while the clock
Crept close to midnight. Thick upon the lawn
As fallen leaves—& in the trees as well—
These psychopomps had lingered past their date
At least a month in order to outwait
Her journey through the elder jaws of hell.

Above her in the attic surged a voice
Like primal ocean threatening some shore
Lost past recalling. When she tried the door,
It took the merest moment for that choice
To be the last she ever made . . . yet still
Her power passed that night, & by her will.

XII. Resemblance

Long after that dark autumn, when the scars
Had mostly faded on what stock remained,
& folks no longer shuddered at the stars
On certain dates, old Zebulon explained
The prophecy they'd all mistook that day
When Wizard Whateley praised his daughter's child
So lately born. Zeb's neighbors turned away—
The tale was rambling, & his eyes were wild
With understanding few in Dunwich shared.
Far fewer wished to, for he knew the rite
Of May-Eve well: the gate that it prepared
In mortal flesh to welcome final night,
& what had stood at bay without disguise
Upon that summit . . . *with its mother's eyes*.

VII.

IN THE YADDITH TIME

"He had seen Yaddith, yet retained his mind,
And come back safely from the Ghooric zone . . ."

—H. P. Lovecraft, "Alienation"

I. [The Long Waiting]

Beyond the pallid sparks of wholesome space,
lost Yaddith drifts forever in her void
of primal nightmare, temple to a race
whose lightest thoughts might leave a world destroyed.
The venom of such dreaming, crystallized,
they wove in matrices to keep it whole
against long journeying—& then devised
an embassy of Wyrms to core the soul
from one ill-omened planet. Drilling deep
in ruddy rock, these minions carved a fane
to guard their charge until the stars again
brought forth their masters' will. Now, coiled in sleep
of centuries, they wait within that gloom
for some faint touch upon the latch of doom.

II. The Finding

They waited for us in a cave on Mars,
beneath lost oceans of dread empires past,
within a cavern echoing & vast
as human ignorance. Far stranger stars
than humble Sol had spawned those crystals dark
with bitter prophecy . . . the chill intent

of Powers plotting eons to invent
each facet of damnation. Still, no mark
upon them spoke of danger clear enough
to warn us off; & thus it was we came
like slaughter lambs to marvel at that frame
of twisted yellow metal holding rough-
cut stones in latticework of alien make.
This was our first—& mankind's last—mistake.

III. The Recognition

We ran to fetch our captain left behind
with mechanoids to measure, map, & plot
for colonists to come. Were we so blind?
Cruel hindsight whispers so; but we were not,
except as fate's hand painted us. No sign
of madness marred our leader then: he spoke
of faring outward, nothing more malign—
until that fatal moment when he broke
away alone, too eager for that place.
Though they hung mute before, the crystals rang
to welcome him as though some wind of space
now gusted through their frame . . . & as they sang,
a savage gladness kindled in his eyes.
We fled & left our captain with his prize.

IV. [The First Visions]

Beneath a moonless sky of molten jet,
amid the jagged fangs of ruined towers,
a robed procession winds . . . with forms not ours,
& lemur eyes of deepest violet . . .
A Singing rises from the very air
(which is not air, nor anything men breathe):
one hundred thousand tongues, so fine & rare
& rich with wisdom . . . *listen, & believe* . . .

So falls the first seed onto fertile soil
long promised to the darkness, & that end
all human striving struggles to pretend
will never come. Beyond such senseless toil,
the Sleepers in their burrows wake at last
to seize this dreaming mind & hold it fast.

V. The First Sacrifice

We'd barely reached the surface when they came:
quake tremors rippling underfoot like some
great beast aroused from slumber. We froze numb
one fatal moment—then young Waite, whose fame
in xeno-geologic circles made
him curious past caution, turned again
& clambered down that noisome hole. Afraid
for him & for our captain, we rushed then

to rescue both, but found the passage blocked
by freshly tumbled heaps of Martian stone
& Waite crushed dead. Our captain stood alone
clutching that crystal frame. As we gaped, shocked,
he swore the price was cheap for what he'd learned—
& in his eyes, inhuman power burned.

VI. A Fatal Flaw

Surely they must have known; the ones who chose
him for command, at least. They ran more tests
than Solomon reborn to find the best
& fittest, soundest, sanest. Madness grows
like any other malady: in genes
these most ingenious fools read like a book
of Holy Writ, & from that scripture took
false comfort in deciding by such means.

They spared no thought for tired antiquities
like Evil, or the doom of Destiny
worked out in willing flesh. Philosophy
& faith alike dismissed, such men as these
perceive the pieces, yet deny the whole—
the subtle poison of a tainted soul.

VII. The Departure

Our captain was the first of us aboard,
for while we mourned our comrade's death, he sealed
the shuttle's lock behind him—then ignored
our calls for hours. Madness long concealed
soon flowered in the wreckage of our ship's
controls as Engineering, Commo, Nav
became his playthings. Sparking panels ripped
from consoles stole what small chance we might have
of rescue; it appeared beyond all doubt
he'd stranded us. Yet, when confronted, he
denied these dangers. All we needed lay
within that crystal frame we'd found today:
a focal guidepost to infinity . . .
& then the starry dark turned inside out.

VIII. [The Call of Yuggoth]

To rend the flimsy veil of space & time
which serves as blindfold to frail mortal brains
too fragile yet for chaos's sublime
& endless vistas . . . to prepare these plains
of frozen methane madness where our Gate
Between the Stars stands ready to admit
such laggard seekers as might stumble late
upon our mysteries . . . thus we submit
ourselves unto our Martian comrades' will.

For Those they serve, we serve: the stars have turned
at last to bring a triumph richly earned.
We *mi-go* wait upon that to instill
the lore of deep Na'morha's ageless heart
in one who comes to tear all things apart.

IX. On Na'morha's Plain

Bone cold in cryskin suits, we stood aghast
at our crazed leader's promised destination—
then searched in vain for any indication
of where he'd landed us. Too dark, too vast
for even Pluto, space curved up & out
in place of sky behind a ragged range
of fractured granite weathered into strange
grim visages. Then came a crewmate's shout:

"The arch!" It rose just as our captain said
We'd find it, starkly alien in form,
& framing stars which seemed abruptly wrong.
Then from those cursed lights flew a buzzing swarm
of half-crustacean Others, clawed & strong . . .
We fought hard, but our chief nav lost her head.

X. Sacrifice Eyes

Beneath that starry maw, we found a slab
of mottled alien rock, rough trapezoid
with half a hundred stains both bright and drab
from sacrifices past. What hellish void
had claimed our friend, or why, we couldn't guess;
but here her headless body sprawled in gore,
flash-frozen like the rest. There seemed no more
to learn from this fresh tragedy, unless
the answer waited in our own stunned eyes
turned now upon each other—lambs anointed
for ritual destruction. What dark prize
would we be spent for next? Our captain pointed
us towards the chaos framed beyond that stone.
"Through there," he cried, "awaits the Ghooric zone!"

XI. Inside the Ghooric Zone

Black viscous pools within whose fetid deeps
writhed Things our captain knew—but would not name—
assailed our reeling senses. Sentient flame
illuminated temples, fanes, & keeps
where faceless phantoms veiled by yellow silk
penned texts with venomed ink wherein one word
unwisely spoken or by mischance heard
might summon The Unspoken or his ilk.

Thus horror piled on horror till we knew
no law but panic. Mutiny or not,
our nerves urged flight—and flee we did, into
a choking mist of midnight, foul & hot
as devil's breath. Our captain shrieked his hate,
yet he was first to dive back through that gate.

XII. [In Na'morha's Halls]

Within these green-lit caverns coiling deep,
we trace the twisted ruins of a soul
predestined by our Yaddith lords to reap
forbidden wisdom's whirlwind past control
of mortal flesh & mind. Mere sacrifice
no longer pays the freight of fated change,
yet turns his journey terrible & strange
enough to justify (for us) that price.

Secluded now in our subzero fane,
our task begins anew: to tempt & guide
by slow corruption of one chosen brain,
by crystal oracles mis-clarified,
so that his crew must follow—endlessly—
redshifting phantoms of insanity.

XIII. Between Strange Stars

Waking alone, I found the hallways filled
with otherworldly vapors: indigo
shot through by brilliant shafts of sound that shrilled
& rasped along each nerve. What made that glow
(sealed as we were—I thought—in orbit's night)
perturbed my puzzled mind until I sought
our ship's sole viewport cubicle . . . & caught
a glimpse at last of our uncanny plight.

No ordinary void stretched past its pane,
but multi-hued abysses thick with things
which writhed through angled space, or flew on wings
of twisted living fire. I turned again
& stumbled blindly through that bitter door,
realizing we would see our world no more.

XIV. A Dream of Ægypt

I felt a desert wind sigh through our ship,
spice-scented by that more than ancient East
where gilded Death slinks forth with nightmare's grip
from certain shattered tombs where ghoul packs feast.
Sweet breath of lotus whispered pleasure . . . yet
my flesh recoiled as from a cobra's kiss
& woke me trembling, trying to forget
some lurking half-glimpsed horror in the mists

of my exhausted mind. To clear my head,
I stumbled out—& found the corridor
asquirm with hieroglyphs. Our captain stood
still scrawling with one finger, in fresh blood
I *hoped* was his. Blanching, I asked what for.
"The Messenger awaits," was all he said.

XV. The Messenger

We rode the shuttle down to what first seemed
a sterile desert world whose suns & sky
& sand all shimmered like some evil dream,
bewildering our irritated eyes
while calling up phantasms from our minds.
The flame-robed cryptic figure who appeared
out of a sudden storm which left us blind
with dust & gasping for our lives was clearly
one of these—until our captain fell
on bended knee before this apparition,
abject as any pilgrim on a mission
to save his soul from ignorance's hell.
"The Messenger?" I queried. *"Yes, the same . . ."*
Our knees all failed us, too, from fear & shame.

Twisted in Dream

XVI. Into the Red Land

How long we wandered on those haunted sands
I never knew for sure, nor risked a guess
at all my surely shattered consciousness
hallucinated there. In taloned hands
more skeleton than flesh, this Messenger
clutched instruments of alien design
& spoke at length of them, both what they were
& how best used (dear God!)—yet still our minds
revolted against knowing what he did.
At last we staggered up one twisted dune
which writhed like some great worm beneath our feet,
& squinting in the twin suns' hellish heat
beheld an ebon structure wrought of runes
& shifting shadows: the Black Pyramid.

XVII. The Walls of Prophecy

Still following the Messenger, we crept
through passageways within that pyramid
inscribed with imagery which howled & wept
& writhed with some weird history. What did
it mean? We shuddered at our leader's smile
as his sly phantom gestured with a claw
at certain scenes: the violent, the vile.
Writ strange, Earth's chronicle was what we saw.

Past bled into the present, then ran on
down corridors torn deep in living stone,
revealing future horrors still unspawned
which showed mankind had *never* been alone.
A crimson curtain veiled the final plan—
our captain reached to pull it, & we ran.

XVIII. The Price of Vision

Both suns were setting as we left that place
of mythic landscapes & lost mysteries
recalling Aegypt's death-cults. Which of these
had made our leader bandage up his face
before rejoining us, we dared not ask.
Whatever auguries he might have viewed,
whatever psychic maelstrom then ensued,
his only presence was a blind white mask.

Some hours later, safe aboard our ship
(oh fond false hope), our medic ventured in
with lasers, sprays, & fresh synthetic skin
to heal the ravages of nightmare's grip.
He left that cabin deathly pale . . . then said
our captain had clawed both eyes from his head.

XIX. A Dream of Home

I walked on Earth our mother, sweetly green
as legend paints her, clean in sea & sky,
with birdsong in the branches like a cry
of paradise regained . . . until that scene
dream-shifted into chaos. Sudden night
spread shadowwings in one vast inky smear,
erasing daylight as a shriek of fear
arose from every throat: *the stars turn right!*

Mild seas brewed tempests then, & skies split wide,
revealing such uncleanness writhing in
upon our luckless planet from Outside
that men ran mad. Half leaping from my skin
with terror I awoke—to find our crew
all shared my nightmare, screaming it was true.

XX. Lost Celaeno

Among the clustered sister Pleiades
shines one whose fourth world holds a plundered store
of esoteric wisdom, such weird lore
as gods might whisper—or a madman seize.
The latter led our crew, & so we came
trespassing over centuries of dust
through alien archives bound in gold, or rust,
or crystal . . . or soft skins we feared to name.

Our instruments revealed no other lives
within this labyrinth, & yet it seemed
that shapes slipped past the corners of our eyes.
Too vaporous & faint to analyze,
we knew them still as marvels men once dreamed,
& wondered at the ways that myth survives.

XXI. The Fate of Wisdom

We searched & scavenged hour after hour
down every legend-haunted corridor
of that great library, in quest of power
torn from the lips of wizards at hell's door
on half a thousand worlds. What earthly use
such texts might be to one forever blind,
we could not guess; yet fetched without excuse,
fearing the shadows of our captain's mind.

He crouched outside, a great wyrm on his hoard,
clutching at tablets of cuneiform
he tried to read with fingertips. Ignored,
we added still more findings to that swarm—
then watched it crumble into scraps & clay
as spectral winds blew wisdom's dust away.

XXII. [The Will of Yaddith]

As Earth's first masters harnessed shoggoth-kind
to raise aquatic citadels of stone,
compelling by the power of their minds
the transmutation into flesh & bone
of protoplasmic nightmares . . . so We too
compel the onset of unending change
in this our chosen instrument. Deranged
already by his fate, he will not do
as human in the fleeting time remaining.
To sound that final triumph of the void,
to gaze upon all mortal dreams destroyed,
there can be neither flinching nor constraining
the will of Yaddith worked upon this clay
predestined from its birth for blackest days.

XXIII. The Crystal Wind

The crystals had hung silent for so long,
they troubled no one but our engineer
who sometimes—deep in liquor—claimed to hear
their whisperings of some unearthly song
behind his section's door. No breath of air
could breach that hardened bulkhead; yet one night,
we knew that *something* had. Wild peals of fright
& cosmic chaos, madness & despair
rang through the ship until we ran to see

these terrors for ourselves. Our captain swayed
before the alien clamor like a snake
transfixed before its flautist . . . & to make
our fear complete, his supple frame displayed
no hint of bone where human bones should be.

XXIV. Where Black Stars Rise

He claimed his healing lay where black stars rise
at eventide, above a shrouded lake
whose tattered phantoms stalk & cloud-waves break
upon a shore not meant for human eyes
to look upon . . . & ever live content
again. Our captain spoke in riddles now
so frequently we'd ceased to wonder how
these insights came to him, or what he meant
by telling us. Our navigator dead,
we had no means to guess this destination
until we woke to view—just as he'd said—
a planetscape of such unreal sensations,
all logic paled beneath that bleeding sky
whose primary was Taurus's mad eye.

XXV. A Dream of Sisters

We made our camp beside those haunted waters,
our tent domes sealed up tight; & still I dreamed
I wandered in the lake-mists with two daughters
of some lost ancient king. As moonlight gleamed
across their faces veiled by yellow silk,
they murmured of Carcosa & Hali,
Aldones & his foredoomed dynasty.
I comprehended nothing, yet this talk
felt somehow both familiar & malign:
a distant family secret, or a play
half overheard. They spoke as though I, too,
would know my role before this night was through;
& whispered as they faded into day,
"Remember that you bear our father's Sign."

XXVI. The Restoration

I woke with trembling fingers clutched around
the oval of some void-dark artifact
which bore a single jaundiced glyph. No sound
escaped my lips, & yet the simple act
of finding this aroused our entire camp
to frantic action. Stumbling from his tent,
our captain caught my hands—his grip as damp
& boneless as a corpse's, with the scent
of burgeoning corruption. Wretched, sick,

I dropped my find & watched him snatch it close,
retreating to that lake where cloud wraiths rose.
We found him later, staring into slick
& viscous waters with *twin pools of black . . .*
Not eyes; not something human looking back.

XXVII. Sight Past Sight

Our medic vowed that he would understand
not only how, but what those black pits saw;
what made their owner rave & wrench his hands
in arcane gestures. One night, voice rasped raw
with prophecy, our captain spoke out clear:
if any cared to share his sight past sight,
he had a method now to grant them Light.
Our medic raised his hand to volunteer—
just harmless herbs, he claimed, a simple tea
the captain brewed himself, then meditation;
but soon he shrieked of things that Should Not Be,
of watchers in the void, & strange damnations.
These visions ended on a gurgling note.
Next morning, we found out he'd slashed his throat.

XXVIII. Sounds of Change

We never saw what tore the cameras down;
but one by one, their bridge screens flickered out.
Our engineer, investigating, found
a dark & nauseous ichor smeared about
the ruins of a dozen. After that,
we took our orders over intercom,
achieving nearly philosophic calm
by means of sedatives. If some great bat
should shriek till panels blew & eardrums burned,
or syllables slurred up from mucous depths,
we hastened to obey our captain's voice
however weirdly varied—for we'd learned
from glimpses too mind-searing to forget
that listening was much the safer choice.

XXIX. A Dream of Prophecy

I dreamed of waking to a voice I knew:
our navigator's, once; yet sadly changed
since that bleak day when claw-winged Others flew
from Yuggoth's gate & left her . . . *rearranged,
not dead,* she claimed. Half prisoner, half guest,
a disembodied brain within a case
which *mi-go* use for specimens, she'd pressed
beyond all limits of mere time & space
as witness to her captors' chronic thirst

for knowledge, conquest—yes, & exploitation
of countless worlds, our Earth among the worst.
This seemed a hideous incarceration;
yet as I cursed its alien design,
she swore she still preferred her fate to mine.

XXX. The Mutineers

They begged me to stand with them. I refused
not out of loyalty, but nameless fear
which worried at our footsteps, & infused
the very air we breathed. Our engineer,
too practical for phantoms, only scoffed.
The captain was incompetent, he said;
they'd seize the ship, & see that madman dead.
I watched his laser carbine, held aloft
like Caesar's eagles, lead them all away . . .
ten breathless minutes later came a roar
like nothing mortal from our captain's door,
then shrieking like a demon-pack at play.
Now I leave ration packets twice a day
for mindless horrors who are men no more.

XXXI. Minions of Chaos

Their rations went unclaimed for several days
before I finally dared investigate
whatever further cruelties ill fate
had dealt my former comrades. Through a maze
of twisted pipes and wiring warped past use,
I traced their faint & maddening refrain:
were these still human voices, though insane,
or mutant prodigies of gene abuse?

At length, a swirling haze of alien tints
sealed off one corridor, as though by force.
Behind it capered parodies of men
who sang & piped & wept . . . then sang again,
until I felt stars faltering off course
with every syllable's soul-withering hints.

XXXII. A Dream of Entropy

Alone beyond real sanity, I keep
a weapon close at hand, burn every light
around the clock . . . & struggle not to sleep
till raw exhaustion triumphs over fright,
dragging my ravaged consciousness past night's
event horizon. Silence drains away
into that howling vortex, as both right
& order vanish. One vain speck of clay!

I know myself as merely that—the last
such speck remaining in this ruined shell
adrift between a history now lost
& one not meant for man. It's just as well
I dream so seldom anymore: the veil
of Being wears too thin now, & too frail.

XXXIII. [Yaddith's Witness]

That fragile candle called the mortal mind
extinguishes so very easily . . .
now only one remains still fit to be
fair witness to our master's last design
unraveling toward its triumphant state
of perfect chaos. Mere flesh cannot bear
such knowledge without damage—thus, we fear
lest stubborn primate ego should abate
her torments prematurely. To protect
this spark until required, we must rely
upon our journey crystals to deflect
self-violence: her brain shall sleep, not die,
within its bone cocoon while time & space
decay at their inexorable pace.

XXXIV. Confrontation

I woke from dreams that seemed an eon long
to find myself entombed while still alive,
still breathing atmosphere grown foul & strong
with lingering decay. Had I survived
alone, then? Surely not: for through the deck
beneath my feet, a fearful rhythm came,
like some inhuman heart too long shipwrecked
within its corpse. Commingled dread & shame
compelled me to confront the source, & so
I carefully retraced that route I'd vowed
to let alone months . . . *centuries* . . . ago.
Picking my sickened way amid a crowd
of ossified remains, I seized the slide
which sealed our captain's door, & pulled it wide.

XXXV. Revelation

I saw the crystals first; at least, I strove
to focus on them only & ignore
those arabesques of altered flesh which wove
around & through their matrix frame. Yet more
than merely visceral horror fixed my eyes:
old Euclid's theories of geometry
gave way to pan-dimensioned anarchy.
The human mind should not quite realize
what mine did then. All laws of civil space

forsaken with my sanity, I tore
that framework free of what had been a man;
& as I did, our time-worn ship began
fragmenting too. Black chaos surged & roared,
drawing me swiftly toward . . . nowhere. No place.

XXXVI. Voices of Yaddith

No life survives on this burnt bitter rock,
not even mine for long—& yet it seems
that voices whisper in this fading dream
illumined by mortality & shock.
They speak to me of Yaddith First-Created:
a world past ancient, primal whim of One
whose maddened mindless thrashing kindled suns
to be as randomly eliminated
at any future instant. *There.* That spark,
last focus of my failing sight, was ours.
Its feeble death flare flickers & falls dark,
devoured by a thousand nameless powers
rupturing space-time to resume their sway.
The destiny of Man is to give way.

VIII.

PRIVATE SHADOWS

She Hears Them Howling

in that lost beyond
where synapses snarl on bramble logic
where the only way out
is down & around
& through the moon's toothed gape

they are scraping souls
down blackboard night
they are singing in keys of pain
& desire without mirrors
or shame

here all shapes shift
here shadows alone
boast crisp snow footfalls
fourpaw clawed
            & gilded crimson

Pomegranate Winter

(for Kore-Persephone)

Some come down
on their own to this land

of barren willow aisles
& cypress kisses.

They do not require
the cries of their mothers,
the breaking of summer
into frigid shards,
the retribution
of heart's harvest lost.

Theirs is the pomegranate
taste of awakening,
deep knowledge of the dark
reclaimed from the start.

Queens of the more than blessed dead,
they lift narcissus praise
to Sister Moon;
her slender fanged crescent
their only true chariot
carrying them home.

Child of the Dark Mother

She remembers as others do not
our beginnings
curled in that first lost ocean

dim taste
of the grave still gracing
soul's tongue

as she speaks it
language of ancient longing whispered
as dreams behind your eyes

as nightmares
you died of in another lifetime.

Lamia of the Mind

Lamia of the mind outlines
night's absinthe abattoir in coils
drawn taut beneath all linen lies
of purity in dreaming.

Lamia of the mind defines
desire as hunger deified
by sacrificial mystery:
dark god-queen's slaughtered consort.

Lamia of the mind refines
Fear's primal tang to brandywine
bitter & potent on the tongue
as heart's blood new-decanted.

Lamia of the mind consigns
another harrowed husk to morning's
milky dread . . . fresh memory
of elder shadows risen.

Waiting for the Angels

maybe it was rabies
(history says liquor)
likeliest ill wind
from a raven's wing

reaving you from Richmond
to a Baltimore gutter
grimy bed in a long ward nightmare
of red deathmasques

& tell-tale maidens
on fever's bleakest shore
where the angels
who came for Lenore & for Annabel Lee

made you wait
in that oblong vestibule
called skull
while they preened

       their sweet black plumes

Ophelia's Moon

Full moon tonight—& in this troubled air
Her image wavers as though underwater,
Dragged down by weedy grief too green to bear
Except in riddling rhymes. Sad faithful daughter,
She lived by every lie the old rat taught her,
Then strewed her maiden senses on his grave.
Betrayed alike by brother, lover, father,
She rises now with nothing left to save
Save memory. Now Hamlet, bitter brave
In private vengeance gazes up & learns
Too late the law of retribution's slaves:
That every action is a wheel that turns,
That even poisoned prices must be paid,
That not all ghosts once summoned can be laid.

(from a drawing by John Austen, 1922)

Coming Forth by Twilight

For what I have done . . . might yet do beneath that sun I still dimly remember . . . I am become she-Pharaoh of shadows, eviscerated sister to dead/alive Osiris. Canopic jars of Thorazine cage all points of my shocked mental compass. Natron therapy sucks the moon ocean from my veins. Mummified in strapped canvas, resined with my own fragrant sweat, my flesh lies mortified in this necropolis of madness.

Yet flesh is not survival's sole element. My enemies have forgotten this truth -- as they have forgotten even my Name, effacing its hieroglyphs from their coward minds -- but my *ka* has not. Clothed in dream & power & terror, she hunts the nightside of these twisted corridors. She despises concrete & reinforced steel for the fragile lies they are.

And she hungers.

Her hunger is a sending of Sekhmet, retribution past mortal. She wears the head of Ra's lioness & her breath is the hot sand wind. Between the flight of day & the underground hours, when sanity stumbles at sleep's dulled edge, she comes to certain ones who have forgotten. Her claws scythe screams into being. Her oven mouth beckons.

For the *ka* lives so long as its parent flesh endures, & I am my embalmers' masterpiece.

The Moon Is a Mask

that fractured ivory
sutured by rumors & myth
                    Thoth's mysteries
                    twisted past understanding
in utter
denial of darkness beneath.

We dream our desires
upon it:
                    domed colony barnacles
                    promise of water

such glistening
baubles of ego mirage

obscuring by sheer mirror blindness
raw unmasked scars
                             clawed darkside canyons
                             sunless forever & whispering
with certain starving shadows
whose air is blood.

Premonitions I

Night shatters in shades
of Anubis
         of silence
made visible as hunger.

Some vital balance drops
this weighted heart.

Dim roads of another world
gape between
         one breath & the next
as natron cravings
kiss my lips to dust.

The air is bitter incense
jackal laughter.

Premonitions VIII

Some thoughts gnaw their own way out
from the inside.

Midnight's
paralysis of vision twists
tarantula waspsting
stark in the belly
        freezeframes time.

Slow footfalls chime the quarter-hours
cross-quartering my skull
in steel
stiletto heels

or rodent teeth
still craving daylight.

Dream Tongues

Cryptanalysts of dream perceive
night's subtle tongues as one
& wholly knowable:
stark symbols torn
from realtime stimuli

blind sleep deep in stereotyping
hunt & peck, they never seek

past meltdown/Grief & missile/Lust
where chaos gray shades black

where dream speaks tongues of flame
in private, primal Pentecost
& soul sings
off-key image hymns to lost gods
nameless in the night.

Midnight on the Dark Angel Watch

The brightest are those who have fallen farthest;
who wear the night like a benediction
twisted & bitter as absinthe kisses.

Lucifer's leavings, they bear the light
of phosphorescence: decay made art
through hunger's slow & jealous mysteries.

Theirs is the timeless amber trap
of lethal insects, plague incarnate
rising above some ravaged land

                  on Botticelli wings.

In the Night Garden

Strange orchids pale as consecrated bone
Flick serpent stamens over rippled glass
Preserving species centuries unknown
Outside this hothouse air where no winds pass
Save whispers. Cursed indeed the heedless hand
Which brought such seedlings from their lightless land!

Thick coiling vines entwine each trellis slat,
Yet bear no wholesome fruit to any mouth:
Such produce once—grown succulent & fat—
Drew forth assassins from Irem's fell south
To pay in witches' blood & wizards' gold
(For but a taste turned sternest tyrants cold).

No living presence tends these leafy rows
Which murmur endlessly in moonlit chill;
Their decadence of scent delights no nose
Still capable of such, nor ever will . . .
The last to tarry here & lend their toil
Now lend their flesh instead, in place of soil.

Worm Moon

Nothing lies frozen forever:
late March thaw
ferment of festering secrets heats up

the ground more than sunlight
could hope to

& oh the worms
love it

they know all the names & the places
the flesh lace of faces
embroidered & delicate now as details
of winterlong lies
your alibis

faint whispers in this midnight garden
just underground
but rising

Rolled in That Dark Dirt

Rolled in that dark dirt
river polished
& numb as pebbles

death teaches us first to forget
& then
to forget forgetting.

Lean fingers of trees reach
down for minnows
but cannot snare us

the maggots come
as messengers of peace
the worms
       like wingless angels.

Sunset, Dia de los Muertos

Marigold light & copal rise together
crying their primal hope, breaching cathedral skies.

All the tolling iron in Patzcuaro cannot wake
this stale air lonely for spirits.

White as freshly scrubbed tombstones, tall candles
wait for the night, for the calling home.

Kiss of sweet skull shards . . . memory licks
dry shadow lips with laughter.

Listen! Holy bells are dying with the sun,
drowning in blood dark silence like an ocean.

Any rough edge may strike a match:
a coin, a stone, a fingernail. A soul.

Narrow flames tear this curtain we wait behind,
each bright knife flickering with whispers.

I miss you still. Love never fades. Come with us.
We listen for two truths & not the third.

At Lamanai

(Northern Belize)

Dusk comes in a long exhalation of mist, soul surrender to the forest. To the past. Crumbling limestone cliffs remember stepped temples as sacrifice seeps through centuries of vines. Shrill spirit flutes etch madness in gathering shadows. Chaac rainbringer spatters tangled green with the pain-tears of children, & dead masks of Those Before have eyes again.

As rising darkness smothers other vision, paired topaz fires ignite among the ruins & begin to dance. To sing with the pierced tongues of demons.

The jaguar sons of Smoking Mirror hunger.

Viaduct Shrines

Crafted of plastic & tinfoil
a-bristle with
shards of dead soldiers,
they speak despair's bleak dialect
to the Ones
who have always listened:

those nightside nameless
claimers of life sacrificed
to some mad dog
vision in 20/20 hindsight
shrill as gin sunrise
mourning these emptied

              prayers

Gargoyle of Grief

Gargoyle of grief carves
heartspace out of
the soft spots

        siltstone

        guilt accretions

enough to spread
smoke wings as seepage
acid etchings

        nerve maps netting

        a tender point

& digs in deep
not at the instant
of expectation

        but after the bullet's

        taste has faded.

Come the Mourning

Yesterday's sacred embrace decays
to hourglass fistfuls
of ashes
& stained glass
shrapnel too frail to extract.

Raw sunrise
seeps its yellow acid between
the ribs of windowshades.

Bone ghosts come haunting afresh
they stalk
your corridors dirging of duty:
reach under your pillow
choose a last dream-shard

& slash till the mirror breaks.

Mutant Autumn

ruptured sunset taints pale sky
with subtle corruption

magpies assume the song of fallen angels

betrayed by frost
leaves flare into strange spectra

pumpkins reveal their lurking inner demons

dried grasses whisper madness
by the roadside

sly shadowtongues of wind

                    but there is no wind

After Too Long Gray

after too long gray
the rain
seeps through in silences
no sunlit
sounding fathoms

gargoyle vision
vomits down fresh spleen
upon
this sodden world

& grottos yawn
leviathan's last rising
nightmare
bulk of bitter knowledge
from the heart

Falling Away

Unblessed with an evergreen
mind, she watches
the day's last light like
lost leaves falling
away

the wind is becoming another language
remembered from edged

steel dreams & the cries
of raven angels

the still unrisen
moon like a guilty thumbprint

dusk thickens in the wound
as woodsmoke
seasons ever darker vision
last whispered resolution falling
away.

Approaching the Celestial Necropolis

Below the overarching corpse of night,
We dreamed as maggots must of plunging deep
Within that ripened mystery whose lights
Beguiled us from our embryonic sleep's
Eternal womb of gravity & earth
Into this long-awaited fatal birth.

The false Rosettas of our minds devise
A new translation for celestial forms
Once muddled into myths to keep us warm
Well swaddled in our ignorance. Too wise
To keep believing now, we read instead
Bright hieroglyphs of life . . . in stars long dead.

Unfolding slow as fate in coldsleep dreams,
Coiled shadow digits beckon from beyond
Perception's limits, pointing past those streams
Of consciousness which fed our own small pond,
& onward into darkness like a flood
Of evolution cresting in the blood.

Fresh-hatched from our sarcophagi, we crave
Immersion in this rising tide of change—
However nameless, alien, & strange—
As though the Other in itself might save
Our shriveled souls. For such enlightenment's
Vague promise we await this last descent.

If Destiny takes form, the egg retains
Its meaning most completely: Khepri's ball
Of blessed dung revolving in our brains
Like some immortal sunrise sent to all
Illuminati . . . *lost gods! What is this*
Which claims our very visage with its kiss?

Beneath canopic heaven's span we thirst
No longer for enlightenment, but know
Ourselves not as we were a world ago—
Fierce evolution's playthings, blessed or cursed
By this dark *ka* which clamors in each breast
For reconciliation with the West.

Enslaved by natron whispers, time & space
Alike now weave one seamless veil of pain

Through which no hieroglyph of hope or grace

May bleed its bitter comfort. We remain

As shadows only, flawed & fleshy gates

Soon strained to bursting by the Ones Who Wait.

—after H. R. Giger's *Hieroglyphs* (1978)

There Is a Darkness

There is a darkness just beyond the light

Where stars are neither born, nor go to die,

A seamless solitude recalling sky

Above a world untainted by the blight

Of breath . . . where silence is a holy rite,

& questionings of what or who or why

All drop away . . . where sleep claims every eye

For its own dreamless drama, titled *Night*.

There is a darkness hidden in each heart

Which craves reunion with that greater void,

& cries its longing like a child bereft

Until the faded veils of sunlight part,

Revealing peace unending, unalloyed:

Sweet shadow of the shadows we once left.

Gargoyle of Longing

Lost desire calcifies
tear by tear on the stripped bones
some fading prayer left
to ravens

there is nothing inside
but a breath of derision
the merest quiver of cobwebs burdened
by foolishness of flies

what dies
entombs itself in earth unless
rejected even there
despairing

lays down its own slow sediments
of pain & rain
gray lineaments
familiar as a heartbreak.

Crying from Twilight

This is no season
For poets. Twilight beckons
Too beautifully now from every bush
That burns with no god's voice,
From each deep sky

Incised with cuneiform prophecies
On the wing, from mists
Called down by ill-timed roses,

& always those faces
Paler than lost moons
Only poets recognize: the ones before
Who lingered past the sun
Too often, wandered
Among blue shadows innocent & damned,
Blind with absinthe vision,
Crying from twilight.

The Dark in Dreams

Indelible as ink, the dark in dreams
achieves its final form before we're three,
distinguishing our terrors by their themes.

Sleep-fettered in our beds, we cannot be
ourselves redrawn, refined, in any way
revised from these outlines our earliest days
laid down in thick subconscious sediment
since hardened into concrete, hopelessly
encasing us in our own history
like flies within some amber of intent
opaque to any waking universe.

*   *   *

So limited, we each must face alone
our private childhood nightmares, rendered worse
by us insisting that they've been outgrown.

Falling from Grace

Cold stained-glass light of striving froze my soul
When I was little more than halfway there,
Gasping with a hunger past control
For any breath of comfort from that air
So rarified that only angels dare
To claim its grace sustains them. As I cried
Once more for just such grace, whatever share
A woman's heart might hope for, my words died—
Not merely hopeless now, but mute besides,
I felt my body falling free towards Earth,
That sphere of mud & blood pure hearts deride
As lacking holiness. Yet my rebirth
Begins within Her grasp: on fresh black wings
I fall to rise, & joy is all I sing.

The Dead Come Back

The dead come back
in smoke
from her last

cigarette: trace memory
tainting the jacket
you'll have to burn.

The dead come back
in wind
on the stillest of
autumn evenings:
yellow leaf whisperings
mixed with fresh earth.

The dead come back
in words
of confession
denied upon waking,
your long conversation
unfinished still.

The dead come back
in time.

Child-Charm

Five eggs for a child, & five black stones
bright as the eyes of my slaughtered mate,
a blackbird's talon laid on each,
sealed under moonlight, sealed by fate.

Deep & warm those eggs must lie,
swaddled close in a swan-skin nest.
Deep & cold my slain heart grieves,
stained with the lifeblood of his breast.

When the child has fairly caught,
emptied again the pit must be:
barren as my own widowed nest
with spiders' webs for company.

Five black stones for a childbed grave,
blackbird mourners to mock your soul,
one white feather across your lips
robbed of breath by the life you stole.

A Thawing of Ghosts

No common autumn phantoms, nor the pale
Drab denizens of winter walk tonight
Beneath rain-shrouded skies. The moon's drowned light
Reveals them almost human in details
Of dress & hair: no rags, no matted manes
Combed sparse by time. Their footsteps, from the sound,
Have bypassed heaven & assault the ground
With force akin to flesh. Akin to pain.

Moist April raises revenants like weeds
Choking unquiet ground, unhallowed graves,
Until truth shrieks aloud—or in the minds

Of those who seek to leave some past behind,
Forgetting springtime's providence which saves
Green evidence within each secret seed.

In This Season

In this season
of sweet white lilacs & ravens,
I will come to you with a deathbird's cry
on my lips at the cusp of midnight.
I will come to you with my black pearls wrapped
round my throat as your own hands
left them.

You have called to me
from the absinthe depths
of your dreams turned wormwood bitter.
You have scrawled out a hundred
drunken confessions
on the broken husk of your soul.

In this season
of raven compassion & sweet white
lies I can answer at last.
I have found a path out from the shadow lands,
& you shall return there tonight with me
should you wish to go . . .
or not.

Sophie, Dying

The ghost in this room still wears flesh,
though the scent of it
whispers in lilies & worms,
her doctor father's favored sermon.

Fifteen years
of faceless black angels
swarm in a sister's eyes.

Upon this blood ochre Styx,
her chair flounders
as failed artifact,
a ferry to nowhere.

Already her brother
is sketching its memory.

     —after Edvard Munch, *Death in the Sickroom*

Death Envy

Don't call it wishing. Wishing might imply
ambition past recliner heaven, some
small impulse of the will—at least—to die.
Instead, they mope like maggots, swollen, numb
& sullen through this bother of a life,
fast-fed upon the path of grease resistance
requiring neither thought nor fork & knife.

Resentful of the effort of existence,
they idolize flash legends: Dean, Monroe,
& all the tinsel mayfly pantheon
who never knew a gray hair on their heads.
Night after night, they slump before that glow,
imagining the ease of being gone . . .
vicariously shameless, blameless, dead.

Brief Darkness

Brief darkness like a cloud across the sun
Disturbs the weather of the inward eye:
A glimpse into the barrel of a gun.

Suspicion that this world has come undone
In some vague shoelace way, & drags untied
Brief darkness like a cloud across the sun

In thunderheads advancing one by one,
Congeals to paranoia. No surprise . . .
A glimpse into the barrel of a gun

(If only in imagination) runs
The engine of obsession, revving high.
Brief darkness like a cloud across the sun

Proclaims the reign of midnight well begun
Between synapses with a raven's cry,
A glimpse into the barrel of a gun,

The shattering of last stars. Like a nun
Unveiling for Black Mass with eager sighs,
Brief darkness like a cloud across the sun
Soon beckons from the barrel of a gun.

Nachthexen

(Night Witches)

We fly as sisters of the Russian wind,
on wings of wood & canvas decades old.
No parachutes: the dark must be our friend
against eyes crossed with iron, undone by cold
& sleeplessness we kindle with these fires
we cast from shadow. Sudden & arcane,
Death whistles high against our bracing wires,
belated warning to the panicked brain.

The fascist peasants in their trenches know
their Grimm too well to doubt our craft. They name
us truly, yet our commissars are slow
to recognize the ancient signs. A shame.
Although our breath is bittersweet with blood,
they never wonder why. Perhaps they should.

Eminence Grise

The future scrawls itself on pockmarked walls
that stink of smoke & blood. This revolution
is old already, rancid with the greed
of glutted felons playing patriot
among the bones of those who first believed
the people's dream turned nightmare yet again.

O chosen, leave these gutter streets & seek
the paths of power longing for your tread.

Scarred marble in the presidential halls
reverberates with rain & running feet
reflected by no mirror. Mock-Versailles
is crazed with ghosts tonight: pale shatterings
lost as they were in life, while looters swarm
around them—through them—cruelly unaware.

O chosen, spare these lesser spirits nothing;
A treasure past their worth awaits your hands.

Raiding beyond the rest, a corporal finds
one inner door no rifle butt has claimed,
& claims it with a muttered oath to gods
long nameless in this city. Fetid death
exhales Amen: the Father of the Nation
sprawls faceless at his desk, cold gun in hand.

O chosen, know this place for what it is:
your womb of state, no birthing without blood.

As if in answer, flags in every corner
unfurl themselves to winds of other wars
& revolutions past. A gray miasma
of ego, avarice, & hunger seeps
sure as venom through the corporal's brain
until he staggers, drunk on destiny.

O chosen fool of opportune delusion,
begin the farce anew . . . that I might feed.

The Night Priests

(for the lost ones of Ciudad Juarez)

The Fifth World frays along this ragged line
between the peso & the dollar bill
where temples of industrial design
rise up, defying pyramids which still
sustain among their shadows gods who thirst
for *precious water,* drawn from life reversed.

Such craving claims its servants where it can
among the violent, confused, & lost
in history's dim backwash: men as Man
Unquestioned, never counting any cost
while women kept their place, when roles were clearer . . .
the days of Hummingbird & Smoking Mirror.

Maquiladora floodlights cannot keep
the night at bay beyond their grasping gates
through which handmaidens hurry home to sleep—
or sleep forever, should the gods await
some nourishment whose leavings lie concealed
in nameless desert graves or cotton fields.

Though night by bloody night & year by year
these dark priests feed the hunger of this land
in yielding to their own, they know no fear.
The reason is not hard to understand:
where jaguar skins are scarce, a uniform
may prove almost as useful, & as warm.

Mount Pacho

Slow bright water-snake on the floor of the ancestral well. Maya blue sky
arching over the people, their children wreathed in flowers and amnesia.
Holy Week arrives with its tamale sacraments, a last picnic in the hills be-
fore the rains.

> glyphs bled
> on a scrap of codex
> stone cenoté

Twenty feet down. Three thousand years deep. Reluctant to offer them-
selves to echoes, the children bleat and fidget by the hollowed steps. Their
wreaths are wilting. A visiting scholar finally takes the lead, nostrils
clenched against a scent only his hindbrain knows.

      thunder
      in the bone
      clear sky lightning

The scholar's own wreath slips from his head. As he bends to retrieve it, the dank air hisses, constricting around him until he retreats to the steps. To a present clean of memory. In the past below him, children's voices gurgle and fade.

      dry dark
      a spattering
      of echoes

People are wailing as he emerges, faces streaked with tears and rain as they stare into the well. Their lips twist with an unfamiliar language. A name too ancient for this village sacrament, in which children return singing from the shadows.

Then the visiting scholar's glance falls to his boots.

      washed down
      to the sprouting fields
      fresh red prints

Spirits of Caral

The gods were hungry here, though nameless. Lost
Four thousand years, these pyramids still hold
Their secrets silent as a bone flute tossed
Aside in ritual fervor. Small & cold,
A child's fragmented skeleton awaits
The will of Those who sent Peru's first priests

Black dreams . . . bleak omens moaning for the taste
Of innocence to quench them. Bird or beast
Or mythic totem, nothing on these walls
Reveals the form of deity: no art,
No scrawls of script. Yet desert moonlight falls
Obscurely in this place, & winds impart
A tongueless whispering to slaughtered bones.
The Names they speak are safest left unknown.

In a Lost City

The sky is bleeding into night,
& all along black waterways
drift ashes of our past delight.

Ascending like a hunting kite,
they cast their pall across the blaze
of sky's long bleeding into night,

the last watchtower's futile height.
Where are the flags of former days?
Drifted ashes. Past delight

or desperation, wrong or right,
the ones who strove beneath them phase
to phantoms bleeding into night's

oblivion. First stars ignite
reluctantly, & through their haze
drift ashes of our past delight

gone bitter on the tongue: a blight
to all alike who haunt this maze.
The sky is bleeding into night.
Drift, ashes of our past delight.

After the Show at Karnak

The storyteller's voice falls still at last.
Now dreamers clutching flashlights weave their way
Through pillared forests of a distant past
Where shadows thicken. Driven back by day
(But only just), they greet the death of Re
Like jackals at a kill—or one to come.
Meanwhile a tourist straggles, led astray
By hieroglyphic mysteries or some
Less intellectual impulse. Standing dumb
Amid the columns, dim bulb flickering,
He feels too late a gust of malice from
These thousand mouths of midnight snickering.
Soon only silence drifts across the Nile,
Whose shades are sated . . . for a little while.

Twisted in Dream

Shadows of Kom Ombo

When sunset's fleeting brush of Horus wings
Illuminates the tour boats that ply
The Nile's defilement, & the towers cry
Their evening prayer . . . then certain spectral things
Remember what they were when Egypt's kings
Were not. Before the hawk-child fledged to fly,
Or his doomed father learned how gods may die,
They slithered through a land's imaginings.

This click of claws, this massive dragging tail
Whose hieroglyphs scrawl horror in the mud,
Are less of shadow than they first appear.
Go quickly, stranger—raise up every sail,
Or risk the primal sacrifice of blood
To Sobek, whom men worshipped out of fear.

Where Autumn Brings Us

autumn brings us at last into Egypt
arched turquoise
faience too fragile for living sky
natron breath freighted with myrrh & cedar
the frankincense of drifted leaves

into which we sink instinctively folding
our arms across from shoulder to shoulder
each exhalation exiling moisture

autumn brings us at last into sunset
skin husks transfixed by lapis shadows
adrift upon some hidden river
like leaves ourselves or Ra's bark
wandering the hours of night

In the Valley of the Kings

Twilight . . .
these doorways breathe
ba-spirits, winged specters
dark on the wind between death &
daybreak.

Unkindness of Ravens

Slivers
of sister night
shatter the day's blameless
gaze . . . o lost blindness, bitterest
omen!

The Laughter of Small Bones

Consider the laughter
of small bones just under
this fiction of grass

where living feet pass
uncaring, unknowing
of elder lives growing

in veins through a night
of maggot stars, white
& fine as the fingers

of newborn death. Linger
& listen: these voices
rise mocking as choices

unmade or avoided
for lifetimes, devoid of
the flesh to remember

that bright furtive splendor
of breathing, of being
a sunlit thing. Seeing

grass only, you wonder
too late at the sundered
earth yielding at last

to its captives, its past
clawing back towards a sun
too long denied.

Run.

On This Last Night of Voices

Troy's bloodless dead rise wailing in my mind
Again tonight—& every night—soon joined
By centuries of lives my thirst purloined.
No matter that these hunter's eyes are blind
To memory, or that my palate lost
Its subtle preference for any . . . wine,
However well-decanted, rich, or fine,
Before Rome fell: these ears must bear the cost
Of immortality. Each final breath
Swells out the chorus like a trumpet's blast
In some angelic vengeance-chord until
My Jericho is sure. Upon this hill,
I'll wait till midnight's clamor fades at last
To silence that is sunrise that is death.

Maiden & Raven

Cousin, I lived in your shadows. Shut out
From anything mundane as daylight,

I breathed sea-mists & chilling winds,
The cypress hauntings of October,
& felt my pallor strengthened.

My lifeline did not lengthen.

Cousin, I died for your angels. Cut down
In my bloom of blood, I was Annabel Lee
& Ulalume, Lenore twice over,
But never—nevermore!—the woman
You might have married instead.

I was more inspirational dead.

Cousin, I fly in your nightmares. Transformed
By a trick of the darkness, I flick my wings
At the tattered mask of your sanity,
Oracular & single-minded
Beyond the simpering of ladies,
The poisoned balm of brandy's solace
Or versified regret.

We are not parted yet.

Six Tailors

Dying female, three bells short of heaven,
The witch within her spirit wakes at last
To know herself unknown—yet unforgiven,

Dying female. Three bells short of heaven,
She spurns the cassock crows & slips unshriven
Into a sweeter future from this past
Dying. Female, three bells short of heaven,
The witch within her spirit wakes at last.

Chilled Red

She takes her reds chilled—
torn raw from the cellar,
permitted no breath,
no life-giving warmth.

Not for her Syrah spice
or a blossoming Burgundy
bold on her tongue
like a ribald French kiss.

Enophile friends despair,
dare to tempt her
with well-aired balloons
wafting scent of the grape.

She wants none of theirs,
prefers her own bottles
kept iced on the sly,
poured quick & sipped quicker.

The risk is too present
for gourmet pretensions:
let them think harshly
of her, & survive.

She takes her reds chilled,
lest she waken a craving
for what she'd far rather
be drinking tonight.

Blood Maidens

(Castle Csejthe, Slovakia)

There is a wailing on the wind tonight
Akin to maidens' voices mad with pain,
Immortal echoes of too mortal fright,
Lost innocence drained dry. What husks remain?
Only those few which wolves or winter spared.
The rest drift disembodied through this hell
Whose tortures scores of maids & peasants shared
Before the laggard fist of justice fell.

At times one strain shrills high above the rest,
Some thrice-damned soul forever crying out
Its torment. So the Countess greets her guests;
Noblesse oblige beyond a scrap of doubt
From bricked-up rooms she haunts eternally . . .
Cursed not with solitude, but company.

Breathless Reunion

Returned
from her shallow
winter bed, cold fingers
clutch those which cannot silence her
again

Nosferatu Surrenders

ash kiss...
autumn sunrise
like a murdered maiden
revenant whispering utter
release

Sanguine Taggers

Those first hundred years
are the worst:

alchemical
symbols, illegible
sigils of demons,
quotations from Baudelaire
dripping off
the underpass,

befouling fences,
defacing exquisitely
snug mausoleums

& oh, their empties
just dumped anywhere
like spray cans
or beer cans
but stinking by sunrise

sheer hooligan waste
(say the elders' papyrus
whisperings,
leather wings
furled against dawn)
a deplorable postmodern
fad, but there's
no reasoning with
young blood.

For a Deathless Diva

(Mirror Acrostic)

Void is the color of her soul
Abandoned to dust for centuries,
Murderous thirst beyond control
Preying at last on memories
Instinct suppresses. What are these

Remnants of conscience? Only screams
Exsanguinated; a night's unease
Ebbing away to vague daydreams,
Ruby stains. All pain, it seems,
Is transitory—yet one curse
Poisons the pleasure of her schemes,
Maddens her placid universe.
Anguished & vain, she's a frustrated lass
Vanished from every looking glass.

Of Vanity & the Vein

Higgledy-piggledy
Naughty Liz Bathory
Loved beauty treatments both
Liquid & red

Such a great pity she
Lacked plastic surgery:
She'd have stayed pretty with
Nobody dead.

Her Muse Is a Raven

Her muse is a raven:
he brings her wisdom
torn from the moon

like a sacrificed eye,
how dark makes blades glitter
more brightly,
how augury
only reads true
while the entrails steam.

Her muse is a raven:
he cries her languages
lost to amnesia
of history & faith,
all the runes polished
to naught,
all those epics
wrought for tongues silenced
in mead-halls of dust.

Her muse is a raven:
he feeds her hunger
with strange morsels torn
from the carcass of night,
teaching with every
red mouthful
the infinite
value in picking
things over with care.

Diving Xibalba

(Yucatan State)

Blue light acquires the texture of drowned legend
as you descend by regulator prayers
of furtive bubbles. Farther still below
your grasp, the shrapnel of a temple harbors
its offering chalice of a partial skull
fanged & sacred. Jaguar. Not greenstone;
not gold or even glyphs to chip. To salvage
something from this stolen enterprise,
you kick down deeper, gambling on a passage.

Stalactites like the ragged jaws of Chac
Rain-bringer trigger memory: Xibalba
meant *Place of Fear,* no placid afterlife
but a playground for hero twins & demons,
ball courts studded with skulls. A thousand years
of sacrifice . . . or one more jungle sinkhole
no more mysterious than any boneyard?
You make your choice. Greed chooses, & you enter
oblivious to history awaking.

Lamplight sweeps out its second hand though darkness,
unanswered save for silt clouds. When the first
faint glitterings of sacred metal sunlight
reward persistence from a niche, your breath
catches in your mouthpiece hard & sudden—
stale taste of warning fatally ignored.

The gods are demons here. Had you forgotten?
Silt serpent *tzucans* writhe before your eyes.
The next to dive will find more worthless bones.

What Remains

So what is there to say of what remains
After the final clearance of these bones
Too ancient to reveal much history
Or anything remotely interesting?

After the final clearance of these bones
(Don't ask about their grave goods—sherds & beads,
Not anything remotely interesting)
From barrow-chambers chiseled in the dark,

Almost bereft of grave goods—sherds & beads,
An arrowhead embedded in one throat—
From barrow-chambers chiseled in the dark
Seep shadows thickening to barren silence.

An arrowhead embedded in one throat,
The stains where skulls once rested in their rows,
Seep shadows thickening to barren silence
Through solstice after equinox unending.

The stains where skulls once rested in their rows
Attract a random crop of votive trinkets
Through solstice after equinox unending:

Guttered candles, dolls, a sheaf of yarrow.

Attracted by this crop of random trinkets,
The shadows of an ageless hunger gather.
Guttered candles, dolls, a sheaf of yarrow?
They crave instead a proper sacrifice.

The shadows of an ageless hunger gather,
Too ancient to reveal much history
Aside from craving proper sacrifice . . .
So what is there to say of what remains?

Bones of the God

(Cerrejon, Northern Columbia)

When they find the bones of the god in the forest, they do not recognize them,
though clouds weep blood and the fertile bargain stains their skin. They see
only the vertebrae of their calculations. Sixty million years nose to tail-tip,
two thousand five hundred pounds of lost monster, croc eater, anaconda ec-
lipser. Cursive on the shore of their imaginings, it basks in slow light.

> a flash
> in the greenhouse panes
> slitherwhisper

No matter that the forest lies changed, black and ancient. That its harvesters
do not adore the god's gift as it falls, hurrying from their laden trucks to
dance in it, faces lifted to its blessing. The dry cenote of this place still
thirsts. When the god's axe splits these poisoned skies—when mining roads
twist slick and fatal—it will thirst no more.

        temple ruins
        gape of the rain-bringer
        dripping

The Dying Year

Her candle guttering with last breath glistens
Upon the threshold of this dying year,
This silent chamber where she lies & listens.
Six tailors? Not just yet, although her fear
Reflects their echoes in a fevered ear
Distinctly as the rising New Year's peal.
Now shadows roam these walls unchecked, unclear
In silhouette as phantoms—& as real
As reminiscence. Some wounds never heal,
But bind us to this bitterness of dust
Past death's deliverance: so shades congeal
About the fair betrayers of their trust,
& faithless women think to die alone
Among more souls than they have ever known.

Summer of Ravens

They came in April with the blooming trees
no further frost extinguished. Scraps of night
among that pale abundance—twos & threes—
they startled us with their cacophony,

but hardly ever seemed to block the light.

May's lilacs held us hostage to a scent
unparalleled for years, our elders claimed
in sated tones. How many ravens went
unnoticed on such afternoons? Events
slipped by so quickly. No one could be blamed.

By June the climbing roses rang with cries
no fragrance quite effaced, although it flowed
from every blossom's heart like blood. Our sky's
once flawless blue was cracked with flapping. Eyes
like pinpricks filled each tree along the road.

July brought lilies lush enough for grass
above a hundred graves. The ravens made
no secret of themselves, though secrets passed
among their clotted numbers thick & fast
as accusations. Children grew afraid.

Now August stretches cosmos toward a sun
obscured by wings past reckoning. We turn
abruptly from this season's end, undone
by intimations that our sands have run.
What do these know that we have yet to learn?

Whitechapel Autumn, 1888

No changing leaves lament the season here,
for nothing grows but woe in Mitre Square.
The belles of Ten Bells, numbed on gin & beer,
have small appreciation for this air
refreshed at last by dawn mists drifting cold
around the corners of St. Botolph's Church
where twilight draws the desperate & bold,
parading past on mankind's oldest search.

Yet summer dies in Buck's Row—not alone—
& Annie follows Polly down to dust
as cries of wholly simulated lust
are silenced by steel whispering on bone.
Their secret reaper rides a sharpened wind,
signing himself *your own light-hearted friend.*

Specter Moon

This ghost-moon by daylight
Is nothing: a vague white

Suggestion of skull
Under azure, a lull

In the innocent sky
Like a clot slipping by

In the stream of a vein
Flowing swift to the brain,

Or the pallor that spreads
As corruption is bred

By some furtive disease
Lacking cure, lacking ease—

A suspicion to sunder
That bright veil of wonder

Each dawn draws across
The clear sight of the lost,

Revealing if only
For moments some lonely

& spectral companion
In that rare damnation

Reserved for the singers
Of dark songs, dreambringers

Whose night eyes reveal
All this world would conceal.

In Webs of Autumn

The webs of autumn thicken in this light
grown golden with its lowering to earth
laid ready as a grave. Approaching night

is whispering pale spiderlings to birth
in our neglected corners: flecks of things
regretted or recalled too late, whose worth

still weights imagination. Lacking wings
once more, we linger in the early gloom
until its warp & weft ensnare us, bring

a sacramental silence. To presume
beyond this moment contradicts a rite
our blood remembers like a myth entombed

in webs of autumn. Gilded with that light
which cannot last, they bind us to the night.

Acknowledgement of Previously Published Works

Some of the poems in this collection have appeared previously in *Crypt of Cthulhu, Eldritch Science, Midnight Shambler, Weirdbook, Tales of Lovecraftian Horror, The Lemurian, The Worms Remember, Tekeli-Li!, The Weird Sonneteers, The World of H. P. Lovecraft, Cthulhu Codex, Weird Tales, frisson, Whispers From the Shattered Forum, The Lovecrafter, Eldritch Tales, Lore, Scavenger's Newsletter, Primordial Eye, Sidereal, Lovecraft's Disciples, RetroSpec, Studies In the Fantastic, Strange Stories, Black Book, Strange Tales, Dreams & Nightmares, Midnight Echo, Weird Fiction Review, The Book of Dark Wisdom, The Tindalos Cycle, Worlds of Fantasy & Horror, Lost Worlds of Space & Time, The Book of Eibon, Cyaegha, Noctulpa, In the Yaddith Time, Dreams of Decadence, Edgar, Shadow Sword, Pluto's Orchard, Shadowfire, Star*Line, Dark Regions, Prisoners of the Night, Asylums & Labyrinths, Contortions, Flesh & Blood, evernight, Penny Dreadful, Doorways, Raven Electrick, The Magazine of Speculative Poetry, Twilight Times, Wild Hunt of the Stars, Poe Little Thing, Quietus, Mythic Delirium, Goblin Fruit, There Is Something In the Autumn, Rogue Worlds, Contemporary Rhyme, Niteblade, HUNGUR, Lone Star Stories, The Willows, Jabberwocky.*

www.ingramcontent.com/pod-product-compliance
Lightning Source LLC
Chambersburg PA
CBHW051826090426
42736CB00011B/1671